THIS COOKBOOK BELONGS TO:

Cooking with Ms. E

A BOOK OF RECIPES AND FAMILY MEMORIES

EVELYN BRAXTON

Written by Evelyn Braxton.
Edited by Charron Monaye & Carla Dean.
Book Layout & Typeset by Tamika Hall
Photography by Lavar Norsworthy.
Photography of food dishes by Michael Witherspoon and Reginald Hubbard.
Hardback ISBN: 978-1-68564-287-7
eBook ISBN: 978-0-578-98359-2

LP COOKBOOKS
LP Cookbooks is an imprint of LEEDS PRESS CORP. Name and Logo is a trademark of LEEDS PRESS CORP. The publisher is not responsible for websites (or their content) that the publisher does not own. LEEDS PRESS SPEAKERS' AGENCY provides a wide range of authors for speaking events. To find out more; info@leedspress.com or call 323-230- 0062

For press or booking inquiries, please contact Charron Monaye at info@penlegacy.com.

PRINTED IN THE UNITED STATES OF AMERICA.

Table of Contents

MAIN DISHES

Introduction

Evelyn Braxton, lovingly known as Ms. E, has six very talented children, twelve grandchildren, and one great grandson. Her mantra for life is: "All that I am and all that I ever hope to be, I owe it all to God, for He has healed my heart."

While embarking on this new chapter, Evelyn Braxton shares her life experiences and recipes of success through her brand, Ms. E's Recipes, which is committed to supporting individuals during their journey towards healthy eating and purposeful living. Through her culinary dishes and heartfelt wisdom, she blesses your soul one dish at a time.

COOKING WITH MS. E: A Book of Recipes and Family Memoirs contains some of Ms. Braxton's finest southern cuisine recipes with a gourmet culinary appeal, along with personal memories of how each dish has deep roots in family, love, and tradition.

After COOKING WITH MS. E,
your pallet will never taste food the same again.

Ms E's
BRAXTON
Recipes
~BREAKFAST~

Claps For Pancakes

INGREDIENTS

- 1 cup of self-rising flour
- 1 Egg
- 1 tbsp. of sour cream
- 2 tbsp. of brown sugar
- ½ cup of milk
- ½ cup of water

DIRECTIONS

1. Pour flour and sugar into a medium-size bowl.
2. Pour milk and water into the bowl.
3. Mix the contents together until smooth.
4. Add your egg into the bowl and continue to mix batter.
5. When your batter is smooth, pour into a hot pan (or griddle) to desired pancake size.
6. Once your pancake is brown on each side it is ready to be served
7. NOTE: Serve with scrambled eggs, sausage links, bacon, cheese grits for a great down-home breakfast

"When Logan tells me, 'I love you, Mom-Mom! You make the best pancakes ever,' it truly warms my heart."

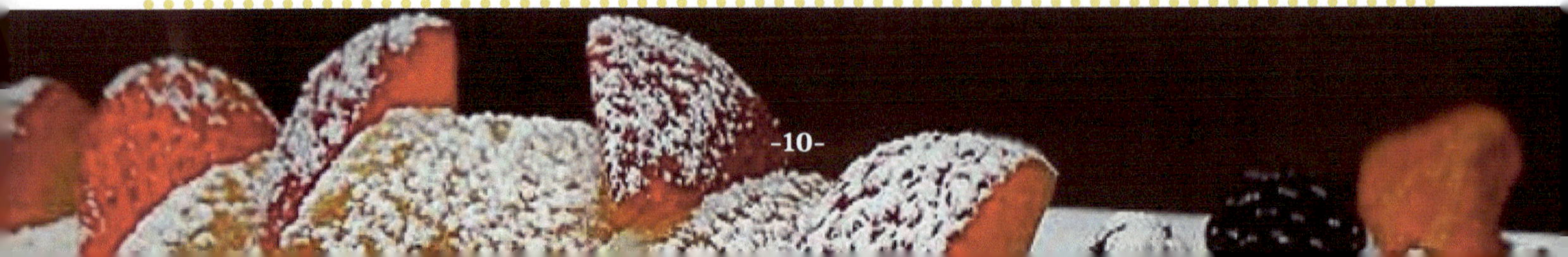

Claps for Pancakes

Pancakes are a common breakfast tradition and my grandson Logan's favorite. He will wrap his arms and legs around my legs and waist while begging me to make him pancakes––doesn't matter the time of day. I mean, who doesn't love pancakes? When Logan tells me, "I love you, Mom-Mom! You make the best pancakes ever," it truly warms my heart.

Whenever I make pancakes, you can always find Logan standing on the other side of the kitchen–– grinning, snickering, and clapping while chanting, "Mom-Mom! Mom-Mom! Mom-Mom!" It delights my heart to prepare dishes for my grandchildren, especially first thing in the morning.

God, I love my grandkids!

My Notes:

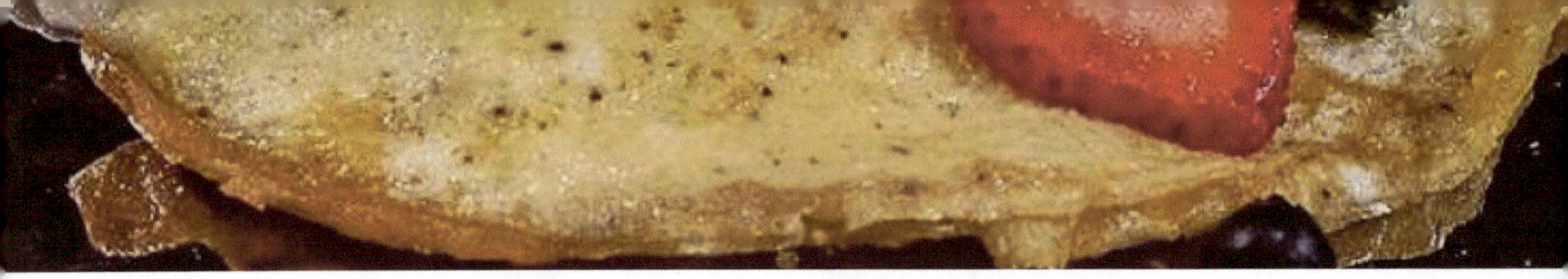

Festive Omelet

"When cooking for my children and grandchildren, I like to surprise them with new dishes, just as my mother did for my sisters and me."

INGREDIENTS

- 1 container of Pico De Gallo
- 1 tbsp. of diced jalapeno (Optional)
- 2 sprigs of fresh cilantro, finely chopped
- ½ tsp garlic powder
- 1/8 tsp pepper
- A pinch of salt
- 2 Eggs
- Butter
- Pepper jack cheese (or cheese of your choice)

DIRECTIONS

- In a small bowl, beat your eggs until the yolk mixes with the egg white.
- In another bowl add all of your Pico de Gallo, jalapeno (chopped very finely), cilantro and seasonings.
- Coat your Small skillet with butter over medium/low heat.
- Pour eggs into a skillet and let it cook on one side.
- Then put the skillet into the oven on 375 degrees for about 2 mins.
- Drain your Pico De Gallo and add 1 tablespoon of it in the middle of your omelet, spread evenly and then add your cheese (sliced or shredded).
- Fold half of the egg over the other to close.
- Put back into the oven for another 1-2 mins.
- Let the cheese bond both sides together for a couple of seconds.
- Remove from the skillet and serve.

What is better than a Mexican American breakfast? Thanks Mom!

Note: Health tip 101 you do not have to use the yolk. This dish will work just fine with egg whites only.

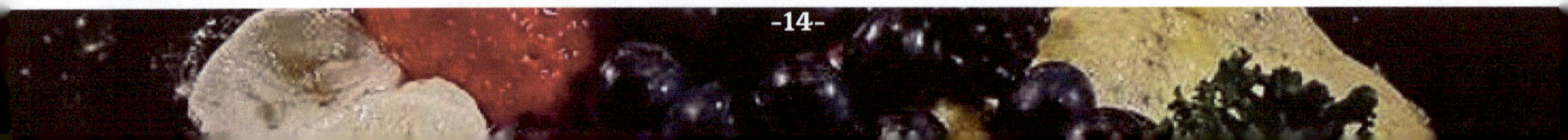

Festive Omelet

When I was a little girl, my mother would make pico de gallo; however, she never knew the name of this condiment. In my adult years, I learned it is popular in the Mexican culture and goes great with chips, burritos, and even used as a topping for tacos.

When cooking for my children and grandchildren, I like to surprise them with new dishes, just as my mother did for my sisters and me. I created an omelet that we named the "Festive Omelet." The taste is incredible! To me, this omelet is not like any other. It has a festive flavor, and the pico de gallo serves as the foundation inside of the egg.

Enjoy!

My Notes:

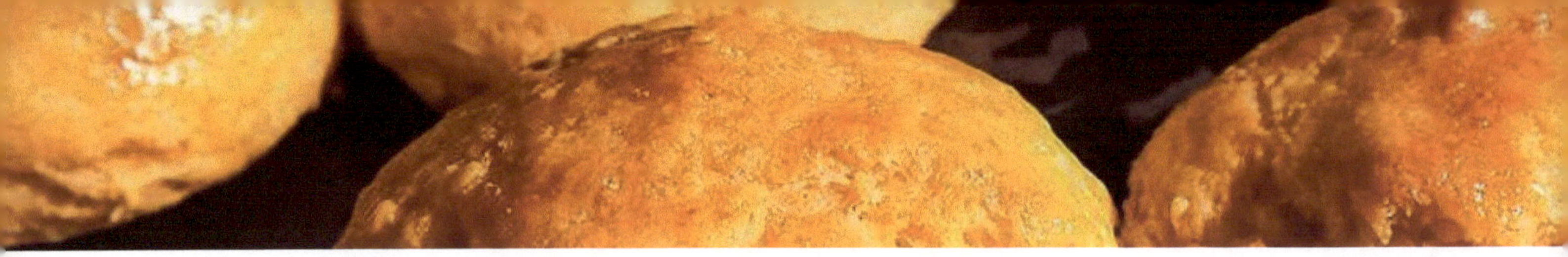

Sweet Potato Biscuits

INGREDIENTS

- 2 cups of self-rising flour
- 3 tbsp. of sugar
- 1 tbsp. of mayonnaise
- ½ small, sweet potato
- 1 egg
- butter
- 1 cup of water

DIRECTIONS

~Step One~

1. Preheat your oven to 375 degrees.
2. Place your sweet potatoes on a cookie sheet
3. Bake in the oven for 45 minutes to an hour or until very soft
4. After your sweet potatoes are done, let cool for 15-20 minutes.

~Step Two~

1. Combine all your ingredients (all except flour) and add your sweet potato and mix well.
2. Now add the flour.
3. Slowly add water and fold your dough.
4. Spray your pan with oil.
5. Use an ice cream scooper to scoop out the dough and place on a cookie sheet.
6. Beat the egg into a small bowl, then brush the egg wash over the dough. (This should make 10 to 12 biscuits.)
7. Bake for 20-25 minutes or until golden brown

After the sweet potato biscuits are done, brush the top of the biscuits with butter to your liking.

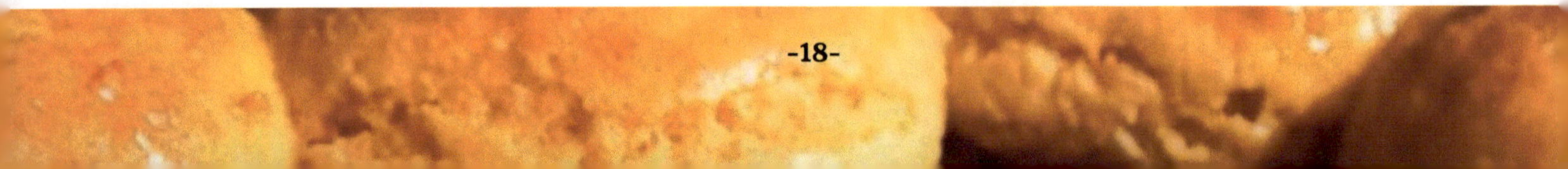

Sweet Potato Biscuits

Growing up, I loved eating sweet potato biscuits. I learned this special recipe from my grandmother. To me, her sweet potato biscuits were the best in the world! I remember my mother taking us to my grandma's house on Sundays. There was always a pleasant aroma coming from the kitchen. Those sweet potato biscuits were delicious and indescribable.

As much as I loved my grandmother and her cooking, her relationship with me was not the nicest. I love my grandmother and am grateful for all she did. But, sadly, she did not care for me too much, and it showed. While letting me watch her make these biscuits, she would say, "You look just like your daddy!" She made this comment more than a few times to me, and her tone made it very clear that she didn't think there was anything good or pretty about me. At first, I would cry, but I slowly began accepting her negativity towards me as my reality.

After baking the sweet potato biscuits, she would tell me, "Here, and you better eat it!" She would take her anger out on me because I reminded her of my daddy. Honestly, I don't know what transpired between her and my dad to make her dislike me so much. Perhaps my mother told my grandma too much, thus making her rebel against me. Sometimes parents tend to take the matters of their adult children to heart. Even when the child has let go of whatever harmed them, some parents continue to hold a grudge. As a result, they take their revenge out on anyone who reminds them of the person who hurt their child. But, as I grew and gained wisdom about family, I realized her issue with my father had nothing to do with me, and therefore, I was able to forgive her.

Today, I am careful not to show favoritism or single out any of my grandkids. No child should ever have to endure the anguish I did, especially when the child had no control over what transpired. No matter what, I let my grandchildren know they are loved, and to me, they are perfect! Since my childhood, all I ever wanted was to have a loving relationship with my grandmother or a hug, for God's sake. That's why, as often as possible, I make sure to give to my grandkids everything I didn't get from her.

As grandparents, we should speak life into our grandchildren. ***Words have power, and just like a bullet, they can penetrate hearts and kill the spirit, dreams, and aspirations of others.*** Let's speak life into our grandkids. Enough children are walking around feeling hopeless and powerless. That's why God created grandparents so that whatever the parents lack, grandparents can fill in the gap. We, as grandparents, need to make a difference. As a little girl, I thought my grandmother was the meanest person in the world, but you tend to criticize when you do not understand. Or maybe she didn't know better. Regardless, I forgive her, and I love her.

I hope you enjoy my grandmother's sweet potato biscuits! I know I do!
Look at GOD!

My Notes:

Ms. E's Words of Wisdom:

"As grandparents, we should speak life into our grandchildren. Words have power, and just like a bullet, they can penetrate hearts and kill the spirit, dreams, and aspirations of others. Let's speak life into our grandkids."

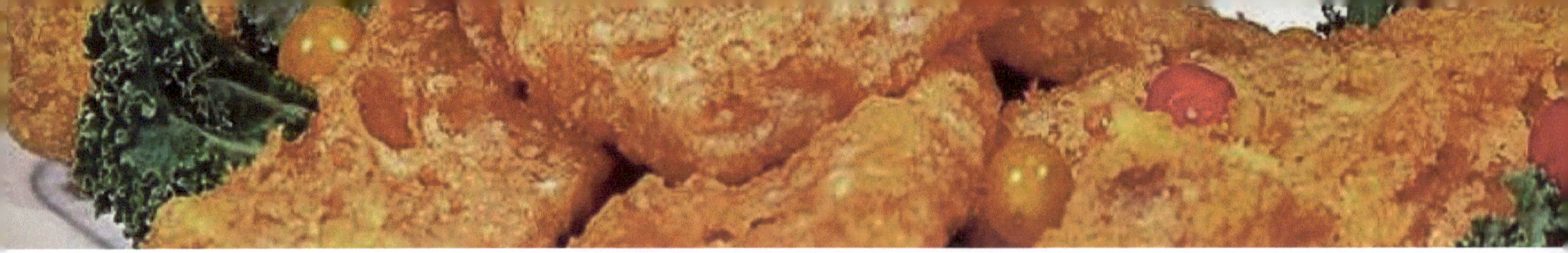

Fried Grits

INGREDIENTS

- 2 cups of grits
- 1/2 cup of milk
- 1 Egg
- 3 cups of water
- 1 cup of sharp cheese
- 1 tbsp. of mince garlic
- 1/2 tbsp. of sage
- 1 tbsp. of salt
- 1 tbsp. of onion powder
- 1 tbsp. of pepper

DIRECTIONS

- Combine grits and 3 cups of water and milk over medium heat.
- Add your salt, pepper, minced garlic, sage, onion powder and garlic powder
- Stir frequently and let it cook until soft and creamy.
- Add cheese and stir.
- Pour your grits in a casserole or any type of dish of your choice until cool.
- Then put it in the refrigerator for 30 minutes.
- Cut your grits into small squares.
- Season your flour with salt, pepper, sage, garlic powder and onion powder.
- Beat eggs to make an egg wash and mix with 2 tablespoons of water.
- Take cut pieces of cold grits, dip it into egg wash and then dip it into flour on both sides.
- Pour olive oil in a pan over medium heat.
- When oil is hot, drop it into the pan.
- Brown on both sides until crisp and remove from oil.

Note: Eat as a wonderful side dish or just add some gravy. Nice and crunchy and very tasty!

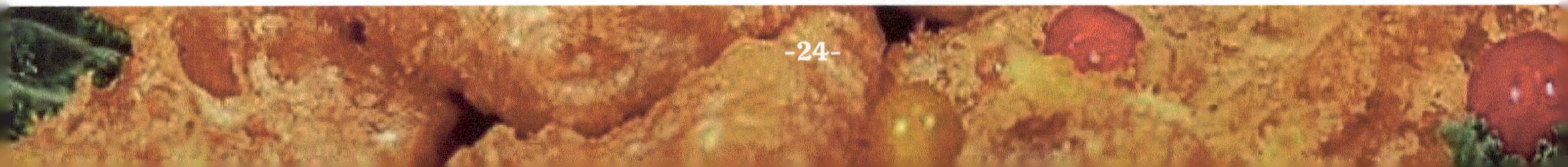

Fried Grits

My mother never threw anything away. If she had a nickname, it would have been "Prepare Another Dish with the Same Food" Mom. Whether it was rice, grits, peas, or beans, it did not matter. She would take the leftover grits from our morning breakfast and make fried grits with baked or fried chicken for lunch. Everything was good; no food was to be thrown away.

Nowadays, people eat from a dish one time and throw out whatever food is left. Not my mother! She didn't believe in throwing away food, especially perfectly good food. She made sure we appreciated the gift of food, prayer, and being alive.

When I make fried grits for my family, I always think about my mom. This is also one of my children's favorite dishes, particularly Towanda's. She loves her grits with gravy. She often says, "Mom, I made some grits, but can you make me some fried grits?"

Thank you, Mom. This one is for you.

My Notes:

"During the winter months, my mother would make homemade beef stew using only the freshest ingredients."

Ms E's
BRAXTON
Recipes
~STEWS/SOUPS~

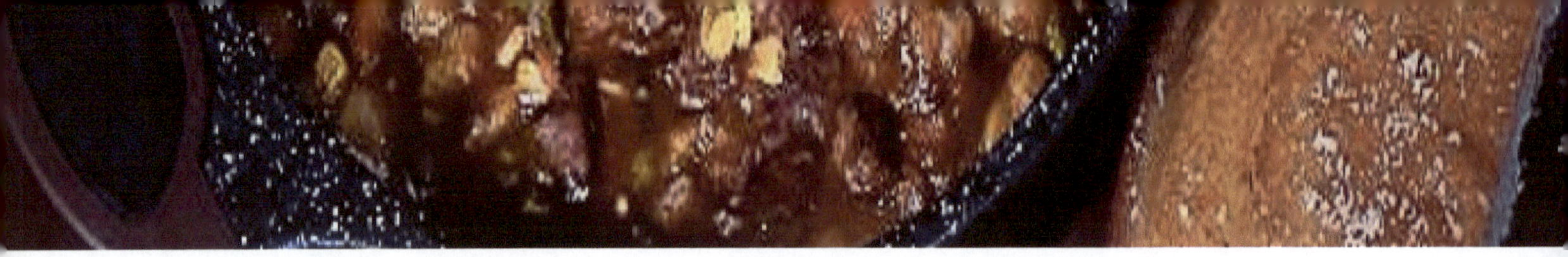

Ms. E's Beef Stew

INGREDIENTS

- 1 pack of cube steak
- 1 tbsp. of flour
- 1 tsp of minced garlic cloves
- 1 pack of onion soup mix
- ½ cup of chopped carrots
- 1 cup of corn (fresh or frozen)
- 1 cup of potatoes (peeled dice)
- 1 cup of beef broth
- 1 cup of chicken broth
- 1 cup of lima beans
- 1 cup of string beans
- ½ cup of sweet peas
- 2 tbsp. of olive oil
- 1 cup of onions
- ½ tsp of Salt
- ½ tsp pepper

DIRECTIONS

- In a large pot pour your (olive oil or grapeseed oil).
- Make sure your fresh cube steak is thawed out completely.
- Season your cube steak with seasonings of your choice.
- add a pinch of salt and pepper, then coat your cube steaks with flour.
- Place meat into hot oil.
- The Pot should be on medium Heat.
- Let the meat brown on both sides.
- Pour beef broth and chicken broth into the pot after the beef has browned.
- Add all of your vegetables (except your diced potatoes),
- Then add your seasonings and onion soup mix.
- Cover with a lid and cook for 30 min then add your potatoes.
- Turn down to medium/low heat and cover with a lid.
- Cook for 1 hour or until tender.
- Turn off and let simmer.

YUM YUM!

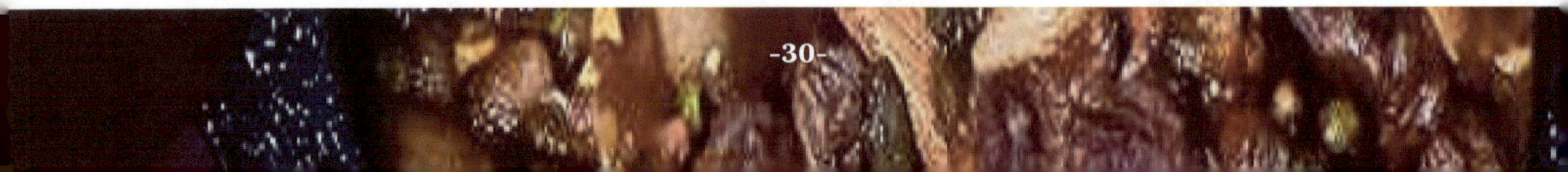

Ms. E's Beef Stew

During the winter months, my mother would make homemade beef stew using only the freshest ingredients. It would take her hours to prepare this hearty meal. Now that we live in a world where we rush most things, I must admit that I cut corners so I can fix delicious meals in less time. However, I still use fresh ingredients. I can recall my mother picking the ripe vegetables from her garden in the backyard and standing in the hot kitchen cutting the corn off the cob. She would always make more than enough stew as if she were cooking for Thanksgiving.

When I became a mother, I wanted my children to experience my mom's beef stew, but I did not want to spend the whole day preparing it. Between my children's baseball practice, cheerleading practice, and choir rehearsals, my time was limited. My priority was being there to support my babies.

For those of you who live busy lives, I hope this recipe for my mother's tasty beef stew will work for you as it has worked for me.

My Notes:

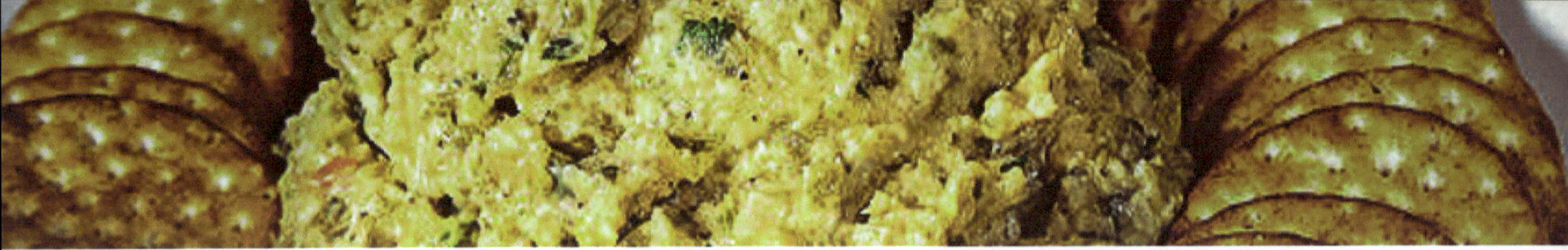

Brussel Sprout Dip

INGREDIENTS

- 1 pound of brussels sprout
- ½ cup of dice onions
- 2 cloves of garlic
- ½ cup of diced green peppers
- ½ cup of diced celery
- ½ cup red and yellow peppers
- A pinch of salt
- A pinch of pepper
- ½ tsp. mustard
- 3 tbsp. vegan cream cheese
- A sprinkle of parsley
- 1 tbsp cilantro
- 2 scallions
- crackers

DIRECTIONS

- Rinse your Brussels sprouts thoroughly.
- Cut the top and remove the head of the Brussels sprout.
- In a Medium size pot add your dice onions, 2 cloves of garlic, celery, salt, pepper, green, red and yellow peppers to the brussels sprouts.
- Bring to a boil for 10 min or until brussels sprouts are tender and done.
- You will know that it is ready when all of the added ingredients are soft.
- Drain and let it cool for 10 mins.
- In a food processor, blend all the ingredients evenly.
- Finely chop your parsley, cilantro and 2 scallions and add to the mixture.
- Add ½ tsp. of mustard and 3 tbsp. of Vegan Cream Cheese.
- Mix it well with a mixing spoon.
- Place in the refrigerator for half an hour.
- Serve chilled with the crackers of your choice.

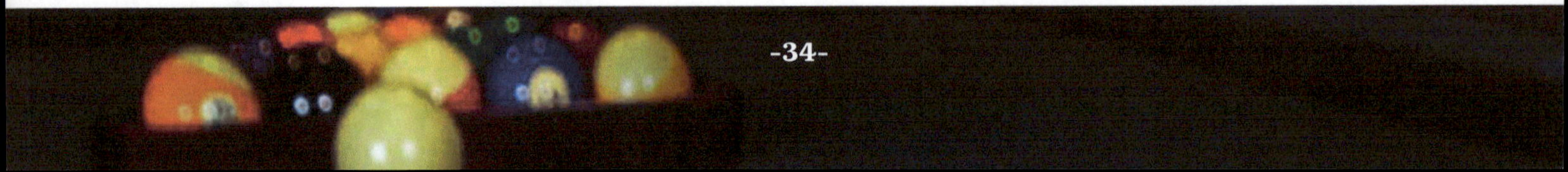

Brussel Sprout Dip

I remember sitting at the dining room table one day doing my homework, when I overheard my father and brother talking.My brother told my dad that he had loaned a friend his rent money but didn't tell his wife about it. He said his friend had promised to pay the money back within the next few days but didn't follow through. I remember my brother's distraught tone as he said to my father, "What am I going to do now?"

"Did he not borrow money from you before?" my father asked, to which my brother replied, "Yes, but there was a good reason why he didn't give it back to me that time."

As they moved towards the middle of the dining room, my dad told him, "Boy, don't you know you are being taken advantage of?"

It got so quiet in the room that the only thing I heard was my brother's deep sigh.

"Son, people can't ride your back if you don't bend over," my dad continued. Then he hugged my brother and said, "Stop bending over and stop allowing people to use you. I'll help you this time. Now, go in the kitchen. Your mother fixed some Brussel sprout dip."

Instantly, my brother's voice became more relaxed.

My mother's dip could warm anyone's heart, and at that moment, it was right on time.

My Notes:

Stewed Chicken

"Today, my children tell me that my stewed chicken is the best. Even my grandchildren love Mom-Mom's stewed chicken."

INGREDIENTS

- 6-8 chicken parts
- 1 tsp salt
- 1 tbsp. of sage
- 1 tbsp. of poultry seasoning
- 1 cup of flour
- 2 tbsp. olive oil
- 3 cups of chicken broth
- 1 tbsp. of rosemary
- ½ cup of diced celery
- 1 cup of onions
- 1 tsp of garlic powder
- Parsley Flakes

DIRECTIONS

- Season your chicken with salt, pepper, sage, rosemary, garlic powder and poultry seasoning.
- Over a medium low flame and coat the pot with olive oil.
- Add the chicken parts to your flour
- Place chicken parts in the pan and slightly brown on both sides.
- After the chicken parts are brown add onion, celery, chicken broth and parsley flake.
- Place a top on the pot and let cook for 1 hour over medium/low flame.
- The sauce will thicken this dish and you can add more seasoning to your liking if needed.
- Enjoy!

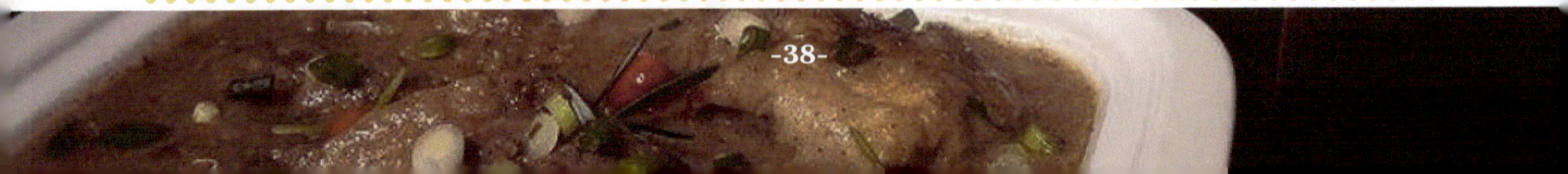

Stewed Chicken

My mother was known for her stewed chicken. She would place chicken parts inside of a big pot, add her wonderful spices and seasonings, and then let it brown on both sides. Or if we had chicken leftovers from the night before, she would just put the chicken in the pot and leave it to simmer for a few hours. The aroma of my mother's food could not only be smelled inside the house but also outside.

She enjoyed cooking for her family and prepared home-cooked meals every day. When my dad finished eating after coming home from work, he would always tell my mother, "Honey, that was the best-tasting meal all week." To me, all of her meals tasted great.

Today, my children tell me that my stewed chicken is the best. Even my grandchildren love Mom-Mom's stewed chicken. I may have embellished the recipe just a bit because sometimes you have to experiment when you cook, but the basic ingredients of my mother's stewed chicken will never change.

This dish is great served over rice and fit for a king. Enjoy!

My Notes:

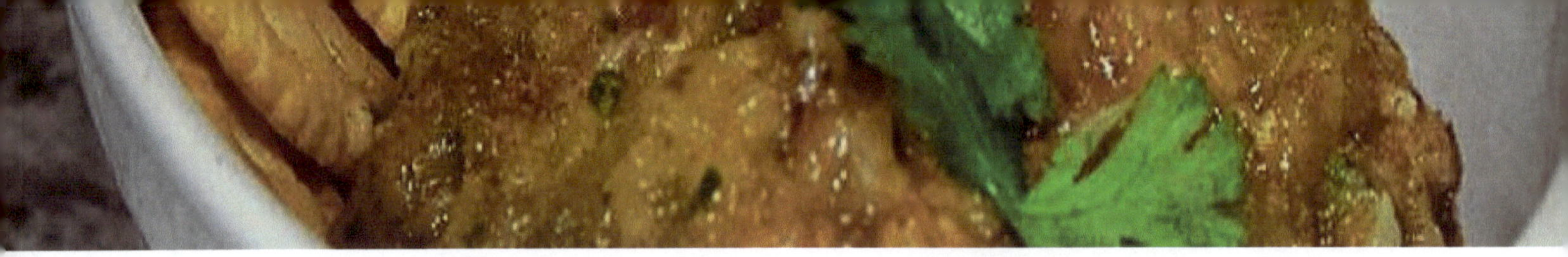

Eggplant Dip

"While preparing meals for my vegan family members, I've discovered many tasty dishes that I wouldn't have thought to make. Eggplant dip was one of the dishes I created, and I have not heard a complaint yet. Once people try it, they love it!"

INGREDIENTS

- 1 Egg plant
- 1/3 cup of minced garlic
- ⅓ cup red onions (finely diced)
- 1 tsp. salt
- 1 tbsp. of lime juice
- 1 tbsp. of lemon juice
- 1 tbsp. of olive oil
- 1/4 cup of jalapenos (finely diced)
- 1 tsp. of mustard
- 1 tbsp. of white onions (finely diced)
- diced parsley.
- diced cilantro.

DIRECTIONS

- start by cooking your eggplant in the oven at 350 degrees for 30mins.
- Take out of the oven and allow the eggplant to cool off before cutting the skin vertically.
- Be sure to discard the seeds.
- Then remove the insides, out with a spoon into a bowl (make sure it is cool first).
- Mix in and add all of the ingredients. Be sure to chop the eggplant as you mix.
- Add a Sprinkle of diced parsley and a sprinkle of diced cilantro.
- Mix well and serve with crackers.
- Note: This dish can also be served chilled.
- Enjoy!

Eggplant Dip

Having family members who are vegan, I always prepare something they can enjoy, as well. Sometimes we take for granted that if we eat certain foods, others have to like them, too. As someone who loves to cook, I make it my business to be mindful to think of everyone who comes to my table. I respect everyone's food preferences and never try to force mine on them. Flexibility and versatility in the kitchen are key.

While preparing meals for my vegan family members, I've discovered many tasty dishes that I wouldn't have thought to make. Eggplant dip was one of the dishes I created, and I have not heard a complaint yet. Once people try it, they love it!

A family member told me that I should add this recipe to my cookbook, and I decided to do as he suggested. Since he's vegan, I figured he knows what vegans like better than me. I hope you like this eggplant dip as much as those who enjoy this dish whenever I fix it.

I hope you like this eggplant dip as much as those who enjoy this dish whenever I fix it.

My Notes:

Stewed Tomatoes w/Okra, Sausage, and Corn

INGREDIENTS

- 1 large can of diced tomatoes
- 2 tbsp of olive oil
- sausage (of your choice)
- 1 cup of chicken broth
- ½ cup of diced onions
- ½ cup of corn
- ½ cup of cut okra
- ½ cup of whole Okra
- 1 tsp of brown sugar
- 2 bay leaves
- 1 Tsp of flour

DIRECTIONS

- Cut the sausage of your choice into pieces.
- Fry on a low/med heat with olive oil until brown.
- Next add your large can of diced tomatoes, diced onions and 2 bay leaves.
- Then Add your chicken broth
- Allow your tomatoes and sausages to cook on a medium/high flame for 10 min.
- turn it down to a med/low flame.
- Then add all of your other ingredients except for the whole okra.
- Stir thoroughly.
- Let it Cook 20 minutes.
- Then add your whole okra, lay them on top.
- Place the top back on the pan and let it cook for 15 minutes.
- In a small bowl, mix 1 tbsp. of flour with a little chicken broth.
- Whisk it until it's all dissolved
- add the mixture to the pan of stew tomato.
- Pour slowly, stir as you pour.
- Cook for 5 additional minutes then turn off,
- let it rest and Enjoy.

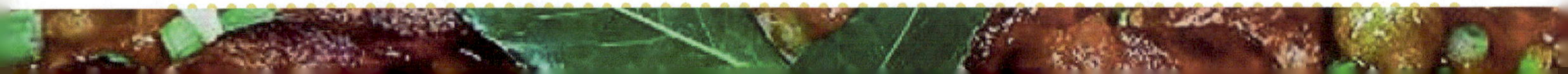

Stewed Tomatoes w/Okra, Sausage, and Corn

My heart always went out to my older sister, Vern, who endured so much. When we were younger, she had to wear a cast from the bottom of her feet up to her hip because she had polio. It broke my heart to watch her slide across the floor since she could not walk. Even after the removal of the cast, things didn't get any easier for her. She was bullied at school because she walked with a limp and one leg was bigger than the other.

Although a strong individual, Vern often cried while walking home from school. Being her sister, I always tried to encourage her by saying, "Don't worry about it. Everything is going to be alright."

"No, it's not," she would reply in a defeated voice. "It will never be alright. You guys can walk straight, and I walk with this limp. Why am I so cursed?"

Instead of giving in to her feelings, I would name all of the positive things she possessed in hopes of making her feel good.

"Girl, you look beautiful. You got those nice full lips and long, thick hair. I don't have hair down my back like you, but I wish I did," I would tell her. Yet, no matter how much I praised her, she remained unhappy.

Later, Vern got married and had children, which brought her great happiness. However, my heart bled for her once again when she lost her seven-year-old daughter due to a pool incident. I remember being away when I received the devastating call from my sister. I had never heard her wail like that. But, as time went on, I witnessed the strength she possessed. I don't know if I could have survived all that she had been through with such grace.

Cooking was therapy for Vern, and one of her favorite dishes to make was stewed tomatoes. She would call me at one or two o'clock in the morning, tempting me to get up and cook the same thing. If I rebelled, I knew I would face severe questioning. So, it became our bonding time––laughing and eating while talking in the middle of the night.

Vern has since transitioned on but will always be in my heart, mind, and spirit. Sometimes I forget she is no longer physically with us because I always feel her spirit hovering around, and I pray that I always will.

Regardless of what may be going on between you and your siblings, if you have any, remember that they will not be around forever. So, forgive, let it go, and enjoy each other TODAY!

"Yesterday was a dream, today is the reality, and tomorrow may never come. So, enjoy the reality of your life today."

My Notes:

Ms E's
BRAXTON
Recipes
~MAIN DISHES~

Oven Fried Chicken

"Oven-fried chicken wings are the best wings you can eat since they do not produce much grease."

INGREDIENTS

- 1 Pack of chicken wings (6-8 wings)
- 1 tsp of salt
- 1 tsp of pepper
- 1 tsp of sage
- 1 tsp of poultry seasoning

You will love it!
Mmmm, crunch, crunch!

DIRECTIONS

- Preheat the oven to 400 degrees.
- Place wings on a cookie sheet.
- Spray and coat the olive oil evenly on your wings to allow your seasonings to stick.
- Add all of your seasonings on your wings evenly.
- Place the wings into the oven for one hour or Until crispy.

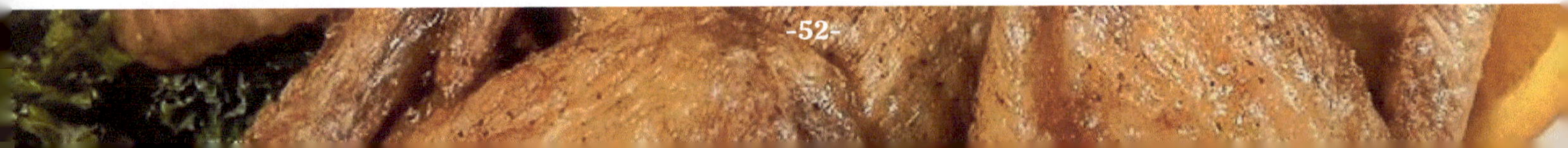

Oven Fried Chicken

Oven-fried chicken wings are the best wings you can eat since they do not produce much grease. My mother always said, "The less grease you eat is better for the heart." She would also say, "You don't want to go outside with chicken grease on your lips."

I remember waiting for the wings to get done. An hour and a half later, I would be swinging my feet while enjoying them. Let me tell you, these oven-fried chicken wings will hit the spot. Crunchy and healthy, your family and friends will love them.

They will taste just like my mother's wings, and you can't beat that!

My Notes:

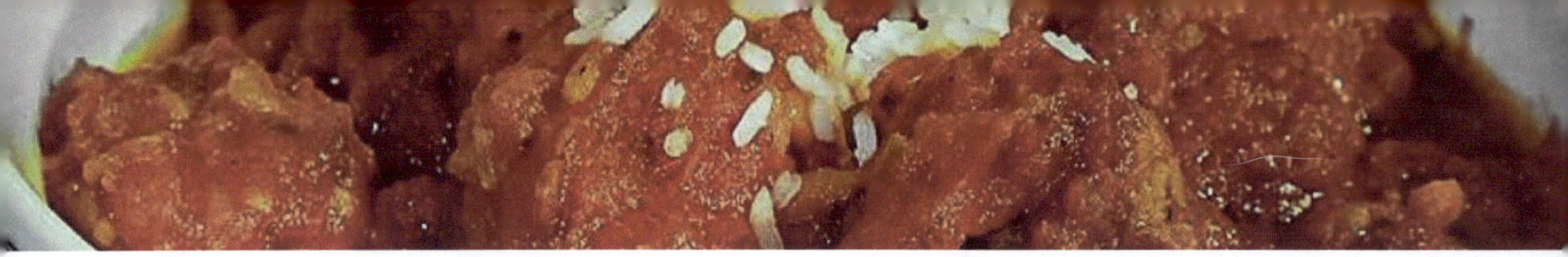

Pourcupine Meatballs

INGREDIENTS

- 1 lb. of ground beef (or Turkey)
- 1 tbsp. of sage (if Turkey)
- 1 tsp. of salt
- 1 tbsp of fresh ground pepper
- ½ tsp of cayenne pepper
- 1 tbsp. of poultry seasoning (If turkey)
- ½ tbsp. of fresh minced garlic cloves
- 1 small onion diced
- 1 small diced green pepper
- 2 cups of rice (freshly cooked or leftover)
- 2 large jars (or cans) of tomato sauce
- 1 egg
- 1 tsp of sugar

DIRECTIONS

- Preheat the oven to 375 degrees.
- In a large bowl, place your choice of meat.
- Then add salt, pepper, cayenne pepper and poultry seasoning.
- Mix all of the remaining ingredients into your meat.
- Make sure everything is mixed thoroughly together.
- Then add your egg and rice to your meat and mix together.
- For the sauce, add garlic and a tsp of salt and pepper into a large pan.
- Roll your meat into small sized balls and place into the sauce.
- Cover your dish and place it into the oven for 1 hour to 1hr. 15mins.
- Remove from the oven and enjoy!
- Note: Serve over rice, with garlic bread or with a wonderful side salad

"One day, my mother prepared a tasty dish called "porcupine meatballs" that left us so full after eating it that we wanted to take a nap at the table."

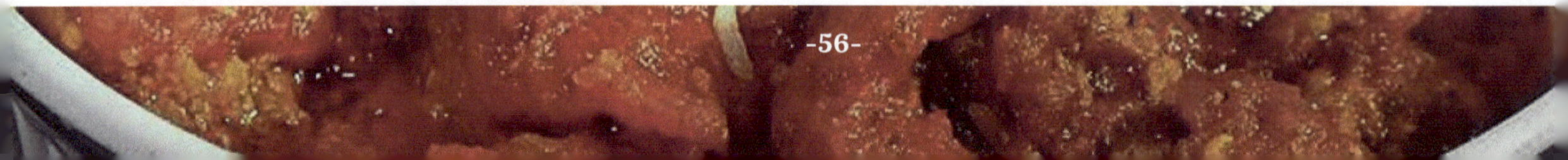

Pourcupine Meatballs

At times, my mother would cook so much food, not because we were a huge family but for the people in the neighborhood. After each meal, we talked and laughed until my mother would tell us it was time to clean up the kitchen and get ready for bed. One day, my mother prepared a tasty dish called "porcupine meatballs" that left us so full after eating it that we wanted to take a nap at the table. You are probably wondering how this dish got its name. Well, here's how it happened.

While we were cleaning up the kitchen one day, my mother took some storage bowls out of the cabinet to put the leftover food in. As I cleared the table, I picked up a bowl of rice. Since there wasn't much rice in the container, I was prepared to throw it in the trash, but my mother stopped me.

"No, sweetie, we never throw food away," she said. "I can use it to create another dish."

I looked at her with a confused expression and thought, Create a dish with this little bit of rice?

As if she had read my mind, my mother told me, "Tomorrow, I will show you what I'm going to make with it, baby."

While at school the next day, my mind ran laps around itself, trying to figure out what meal my mother would make with the leftover rice. After school, I hurried straight home to help her create the mystery dish.

"We're going to make porcupine meatballs," my mother announced when she entered the kitchen.

My sisters and I laughed for a moment before asking, "Why is it called that, Mom?"

"The name comes from when you mix the ingredients into a bowl and add the rice at the end," she replied. "The rice sticks out everywhere like the needles on the coat of a porcupine."

And that is how porcupine meatballs were born.

My Notes:

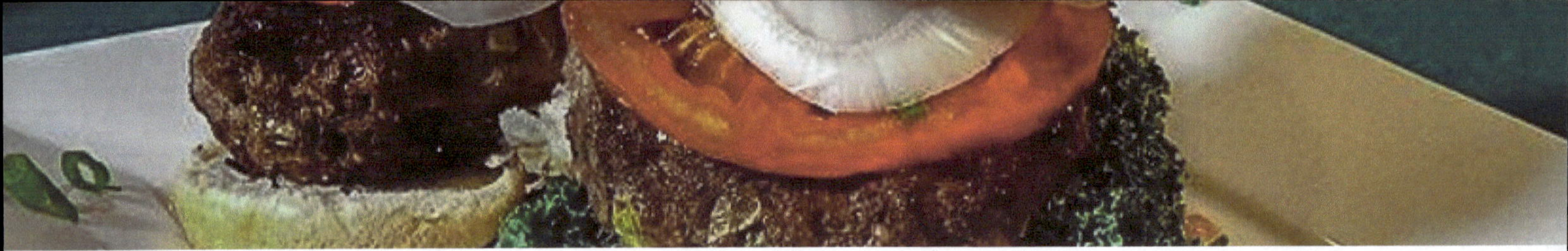

Big Burger

INGREDIENTS

- 1 pack of ground beef or turkey
- 1 onion
- 1 green pepper
- 1 egg
- 2 tbsp. of breadcrumbs
- ½ tsp. of salt
- ½ tsp. of pepper
- 1 tsp. of garlic powder

DIRECTIONS

- Dice your onion and green pepper finely and place them into a medium size bowl.
- Add all of the rest of your ingredients to the bowl.
- Mix the ground beef and other ingredients evenly with your hands.
- Roll patties into a medium size.
- place them onto a large skillet on medium/low heat.
- Cook each side for 4 minutes or until done.
- Covering the skillet with a lid and there you have it!
- Enjoy!

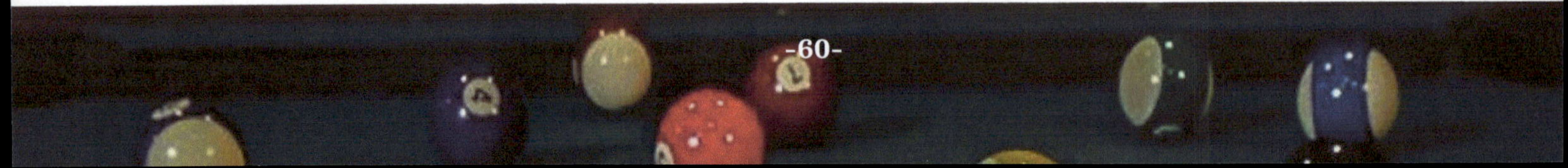

Big Burger

As a parent, I was always concerned with my children eating fast food because I did not believe it was healthy. It causes weight gain and sluggish behavior, not to mention the life-shifting diseases caused by the lack of good nutritional value. Can you believe despite all the recipes in my arsenal, they still craved fast food? If we were on a family outing and my children saw a sign advertising a tasty burger for a nearby restaurant, our vehicle would start to shake from their anticipation and excitement––their little faces glued to the window.

"Wouldn't you rather have one of my burgers? It will be three times the size of what you would get from there and made with love?" I asked while pointing out the window in the direction of the establishment.

"We don't want a big burger made with love," they would reply. "We want their burger!"

Then I thought, Maybe they want to be like other kids whose family treats them to fast food from time to time. None of them even considered if we had the money to eat out. Even though money was never their concern, we didn't always have it. Back then, every dime counted.

I remember a time we were driving by a burger place, and the kids begged, "Daddy, can we go past there?"

"You want to go past there?" he asked them.

"Yes!" they all hollered, excited.

I told him not to promise such things.

"Maybe next Saturday," I told the children.

"No, Mommy. Daddy said today," they replied.

Just as he promised, he drove right past the restaurant. Their dad was a great jokester, but to the children, it wasn't funny.

Cunningly, I said, "When we get home, I'll make ice cream cones for you."

"We don't have ice cream cones," they said in unison, looking disappointed.

"Yes, we do," I said. "I bought some this morning."

Once we got home, they reminded me that they were hungry. I told them to give me thirty minutes to fix a hot meal––a "Big Burger". This meal is fit for any family, whether served with vegetables or baked fries.

My Notes:

Diabetic Meal w/Rice

INGREDIENTS

- 1 pack of vegetarian patties
- 1 large, sweet onion
- 1 green pepper
- 1 red pepper
- 1 tsp of salt
- 1 tsp of pepper
- 2 cloves of garlic
- 1 can of vegetable broth
- 1 pack of onion soup mix
- 2 cups of white or brown rice

"This healthy meal is great for those who have diabetes. Besides that, the preparation is easy. When you eat healthy, you feel better. Well, at least I do."

DIRECTIONS

- Preheat the oven to 325 degrees.
- In a large Skillet, place 2 tablespoons of olive oil.
- Mix one tablespoon of wheat flour in the skillet.
- Add your salt and pepper and mix it all together.
- Then add your vegetable stock (this should make a roué.)
- Add your onion, green peppers, garlic (finely diced) and onion soup mix into the skillet.
- Place vegetarian patties with your vegetables into a baking dish.
- Pour vegetable stock on top of vegetarian patties until covered.
- Place in the oven and let bake until the sauce is almost light brown.
- This should take up to 40- 45 minutes until fork tender.
- Once everything is done, serve your vegetarian patties over rice.

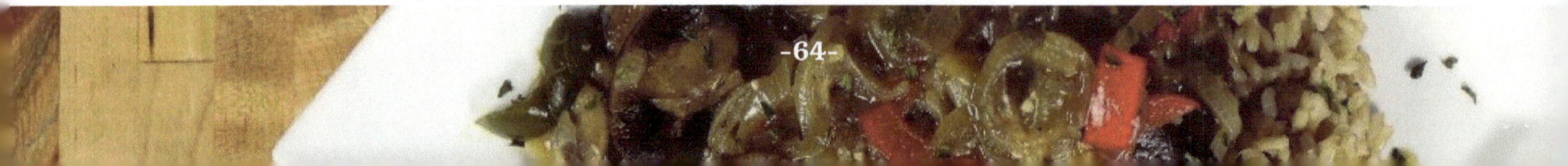

Diabetic Meal w/Rice

Three of my best friends are vegetarians. One of them always asked me to share this recipe with them, and I would tell her if she shared one of her, I would gladly share mine. Eventually, I broke down and gave it to her. I mean, after all, she is my best friend. So, how could I continue to deny her request?

This healthy meal is great for those who have diabetes. Besides that, the preparation is easy. When you eat healthy, you feel better. Well, at least I do.

Coming from a southern background, the way things are prepared may not always be healthy. However, if you are a diabetic, this is the recipe for you.

Remember, you are what you eat!
So, we must "eat to live and not live to eat."
Let this recipe help you do just that.

My Notes:

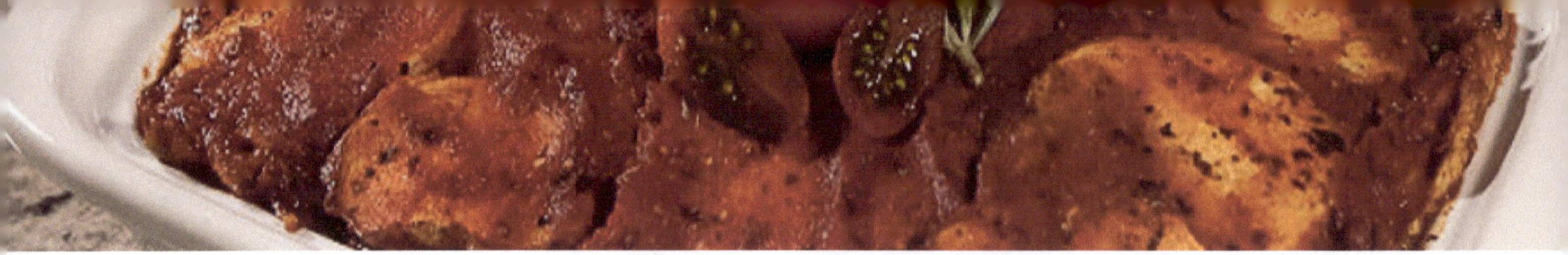

Diabetic Casserole

INGREDIENTS

- 1 small eggplant (cut into thin slices)
- 2 small squashes
- 3 large tomatoes (cut into thin slices)
- 1 small onion (diced)
- 1 zucchini (cut into thin slices)
- 2 tbsp. of minced garlic
- 1 tsp of crack pepper
- 1 pack of vegetarian cheese (shredded)
- 2 tbsp. of olive oil
- 1 small jar of tomato sauce
- ½ cup of peas
- portobello burgers
- 1 tbsp. of cornstarch

"This casserole is one of my favorite meals. Even those who aren't the healthiest eaters love this dish as much as I do. It is just plain ole good!"

DIRECTIONS

- Preheat the oven to 375 degrees.
- Place all vegetables (except eggplant and Portobello burgers) including tomatoes in a pot and steam for about 15 minutes.
- Add salt, pepper, and cornstarch and stir frequently.
- Add minced garlic and all other seasoning.
- Peel and cut your eggplants into thin circles.
- Get a medium casserole dish.
- Season the eggplant on both sides.
- Put a tablespoon of olive oil in the bottom of your casserole dish.
- Start by Layering your eggplant
- Then you add your vegetable mix and crumble your portabella on top of your eggplant with the vegetarian cheese being last.
- Each time you layer the eggplant, sprinkle salt and pepper on top or any other seasoning that you prefer.
- Continue to layer until all ingredients are gone.
- Be sure to place the eggplant on the top of all of your ingredients along with your tomato sauce and cheese.
- Cheese should be the last item layered on the dish.
- Cover with aluminum foil or a casserole top.
- Cover and place in the oven for 1hour to 1 ½ hours
- let cool for about 20 minutes

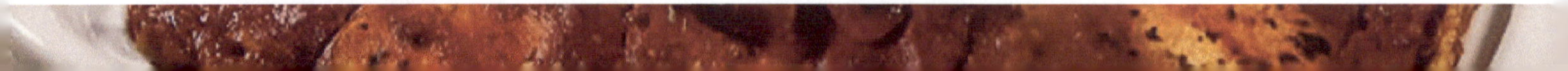

Diabetic Casserole

Because I am a diabetic, I have to prepare food to fit my lifestyle and remain healthy. There are many benefits to eating healthy: increased energy, healthy skin, lower blood pressure, and stable glucose levels. When I think about eating healthy, I often think about the story my dad once told me about not losing your life over a piece of tail.

There were two dogs––one with a long tail and the other had a short one. They loved playing and daring each other to jump from one railroad track to the next when the train was coming. One day, the dog with the long tail accepted a dare as the train was approaching but waited too long to jump to the next track, causing him to lose his tail.

As they continued walking down the tracks, the dog who lost his tail said, "Man, I miss my tail. I'm going back to get it."

"No, don't go back," the dog with the short tail told him. "You don't need that tail."

The other dog insisted that he must go back for his tail because he missed it so much.

The dog with the short tail then said, "Man, don't you see the train coming? Don't lose your life over a piece of tail."

In essence, a tail can be anything you value more than your life. It could be food, alcohol, or even relationships. We have to stop taking dares in life and take care of ourselves.

This casserole is one of my favorite meals. Even those who aren't the healthiest eaters love this dish as much as I do. It is just plain ole good!

So good you might have to hook your chair up to a tow truck to pull yourself from the table.

My Notes:

Stay for Stuffed Chicken

"This recipe has been in my family for many years. It is a common yet special dish everyone is sure to love."

INGREDIENTS

- 4 chicken breasts
- 1 box of cornbread stuffing
- pinch of salt
- pinch of pepper
- sage
- poultry season
- onions
- celery
- 1 can of chicken broth
- ½ stick of butter
- A cutting board
- Saran wrap
- Large mixing bowl
- Large pan
- Medium size casserole dish
- Meat cleaver
- Cookie sheet
- Parsley flakes

DIRECTIONS

~Step One~

- In a small pot pour in a ½ cup of chicken broth, diced onions, and diced celery.
- Cook for about 15 min.
- Prepare your stuffing.
- Take a box of cornbread stuffing, put it in a bowl.
- Then add a ½ stick of butter.
- Add in your poultry seasoning, sage, salt, pepper and parsley flakes
- Now pour the cooked chicken broth and mix it well.
- Be sure that it is not overly moist.

~Step Two~

- Clean chicken and dry thoroughly.
- Cover your cutting board with saran wrap.
- cut each breast into 4 pieces with 2-inch slits.
- After your chicken has been cut, cover each piece with saran wrap and texturize with a meat cleaver until evenly flat.
- After your chicken is flat, remove saran wrap off of your chicken.
- Season your chicken breast with a pinch of salt and pepper.

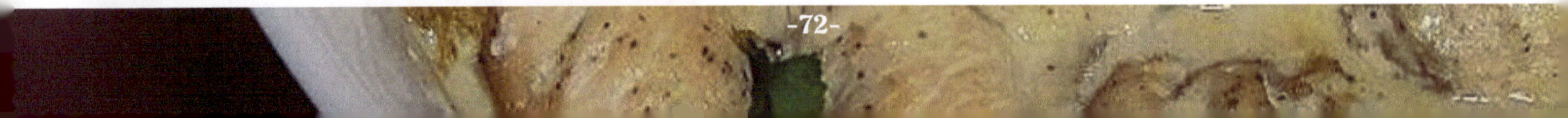

DIRECTIONS -continued-

~Step Three~

- Preheat the oven to 375 degrees.
- Lay your flat chicken breast on a cookie sheet.
- Take a tablespoon of dressing and place it on the end of the flat chicken breast and begin to roll the breast.
- Make sure the stuffing is covered completely.
- Take your rolled chicken breast and lay it in your casserole dish.
- Place your casserole dish in the oven for 15 minutes.
- Remove from the oven.
- In a medium-mixing bowl pour in a can of celery soup (or mushroom soup) and ½ cup of chicken broth.
- Blend together until it's nice and smooth.
- Then pour it over the chicken.
- Put the chicken back in the oven for 30 minutes.
- Remove from the oven,
- let it rest for 5 min.
- chicken breast with a pinch of salt and pepper.

Stay for Stuffed Chicken

This recipe has been in my family for many years. It is a common yet special dish everyone is sure to love. My mother always conjured up new ideas for meals to keep us anticipating and craving her next dish.

My father was a pastor, and our entire church knew our family as a cooking family. You could always count on Sister Jackson to whip up a delicious meal. Every Sunday after service, my father would invite several of the ministers to come by for dinner so they could indulge in my mother's cooking. Still dressed in their church attire, they would sit at the table smiling from ear to ear while the aroma filled the house. You could almost taste the food through the smell.

My sisters and I were always happy if our guests didn't eat all of the food so we could enjoy the meal, as well. You see, back then, adults ate first, especially pastors, who were considered to be "next to God." Thank God for my mother, though. She always made sure to put aside some food so her children could eat, too. If left up to the ministers, we would have starved. They often ate EVERYTHING placed on the table, including the salt and pepper.

I guess that was to be expected when your mother
is the best cook in town!

My Notes:

"I never heard my mother talk about anyone; however, the ladies who came over had plenty to say. If their gossiping became too heavy, my mother would stand up and ask them if they would like more chicken or bread. Homemade bread was also something she made."

Mustard Fried Chicken

"My siblings and I loved my mother's mustard fried chicken because it was crispy, and the aroma was amazing."

INGREDIENTS

- Chicken wings
- Salt
- Pepper
- Poultry seasoning
- Sage
- Rosemary
- 1/3 cup of mustard
- Vegetable oil (or oil of your preference)
- Flour

DIRECTIONS

- First Wash off the chicken wings.
- Season your chicken well to your liking with the Salt, pepper, sage, poultry seasoning and rosemary if you prefer.
- Mix the chicken very well together.
- Add ⅓ cup of mustard put over the wings *mix well*.
- Then coat your chicken in flour before placing in the Oil on a medium/ high flame (be sure the oil is hot!)
- Cook for 20-25 minutes until golden and crispy.
- Remove from pot, place on napkin to drain.

Mustard Fried Chicken

My siblings and I loved my mother's mustard fried chicken because it was crispy, and the aroma was amazing. At times, my mom would invite the ladies from the church over to fellowship while eating hot mustard chicken and a side of vegetables. They would sit in the living or dining room, talking about the church's previous Sunday service or Pastor and the First Lady. Whenever they would come over, we would have to go outside and play. Back in those days, children were not allowed to sit around and be in grown folks' conversations. Today, children can converse and interact with adults in their discussions. I think our parents kept us away from those conversations to preserve our innocence, even from gossip.

I never heard my mother talk about anyone; however, the ladies who came over had plenty to say. If their gossiping became too heavy, my mother would stand up and ask them if they would like more chicken or bread. Homemade bread was also something she made. My siblings and I could not wait for those ladies to leave so we could eat all of the remaining chicken. Sometimes they would get so involved in the conversation that they wouldn't even finish the chicken, which meant more for us.

Other times, my mother would prepare the mustard chicken for my daddy and us to enjoy whenever he came home from work. We would have mustard chicken, rice, and gravy. We ate a lot of rice because we were considered Geechee.

The neighbors and their children would always come over and join us for dinner. I never knew my mother to turn anyone away from her table. I think that's why we are the way that we are today.

Anybody can come to eat and be merry.

My Notes:

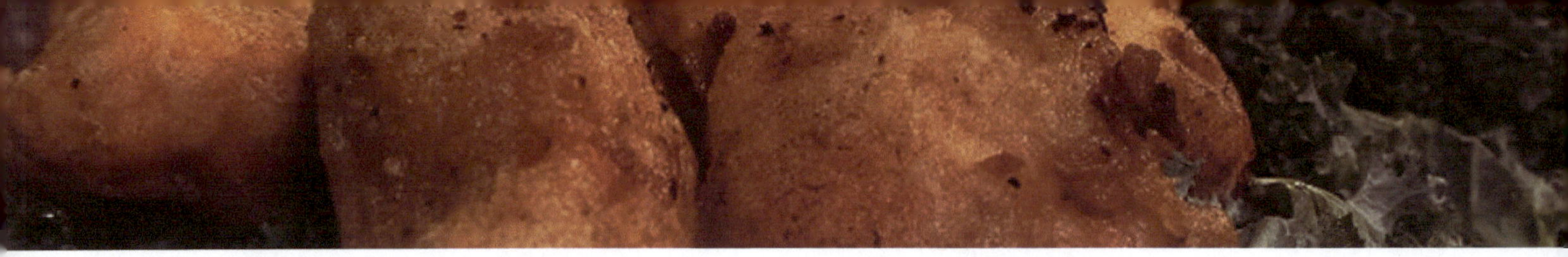

Salmon Pockets

INGREDIENTS

- 1 med size salmon
- 1 tsp salt
- 1 tsp pepper
- 1 tsp cayenne pepper
- 1 tsp Fish seasoning
- 1 egg
- ½ cup of flour
- ¼ cup of water
- Parsley flakes

DIRECTIONS

- Start by cutting the Med size Salmon into small strips.
- Add a pinch of salt, pepper, fish seasoning and cayenne pepper to each strip.
- To Make a batter, put in a large Ziplock bag 1 whisked egg, ¼ cup of water and ½ cup of flour.
- Also add a pinch of salt, pepper, fish seasoning and cayenne pepper to your batter.
- Mix/shake it up very well until everything blends.Be sure to make the batter nice and loose.
- In the case that you don't think your fish is not seasoned enough, you can add more of your favorite seasoning to the batter.
- In a medium pot, fill half full of oil over a medium/ high flame (be sure your oil is NOT too hot).
- Add the battered salmon to the oil.
- let it cook for 4 min or until golden brown.
- Take it out, drain it.
- Sprinkle parsley flakes & serve.

Salmon Pockets

One day, my friend, Barbara, and her late husband, Leon (whom I affectionately refer to as my sister and brother) came to visit me. When they arrived, they immediately mentioned that they were hungry. I laughed to myself while thinking, Now why would they cover over without eating first?

"Evelyn, I need something different to eat," Barbara told me.

"Well, what do you want to eat?" I asked her.

"I don't know," she replied. "You're a good cook. What's something different?"

We went back and forth, complimenting each other on how we both were great cooks. Leon must have gotten tired of listening to us, because he jokingly blurted out, "Shut up and think of something already! I just want to eat!" I sure do miss that man telling us to shut up.

When I looked in the refrigerator, there was salmon. Since we always ate baked salmon, we certainly didn't want that. So, I got creative.

"I am going to surprise you," I told them. "The two of you go sit in the living room and watch TV. I got this in here."

Barbara replied by saying, "Okay. Just make sure it tastes good."

Before I could even respond to her, Leon said, "Knowing E., it will be good."

While I was preparing the dish, Barbara snuck into the kitchen a few times to watch me. It was Barbara who named this dish; she said it looked like a little pocket. It must have been satisfactory because about two months afterwards, she asked me, "When are you going to fix those salmon pockets again?" to which I replied, "You were there and know how they are made. Why don't you give it a try yourself?"

We both laughed.

See what happens when you get creative in the kitchen.

My Notes:

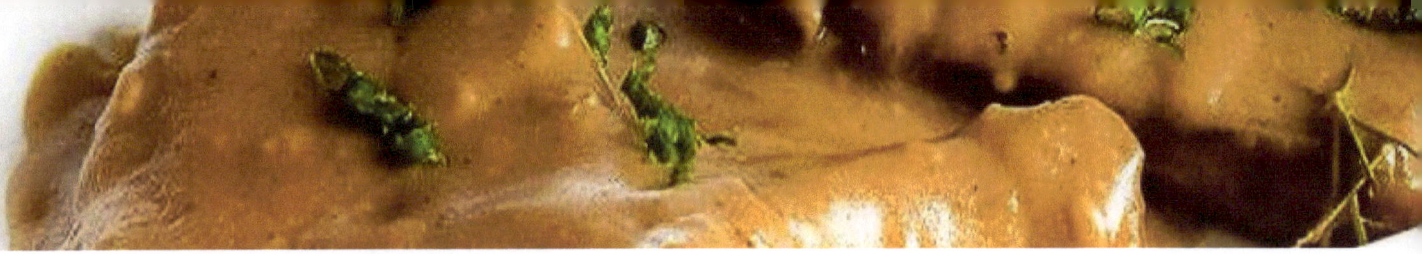

Smothered Pork Chops

INGREDIENTS

- 4 pork chops
- 1 tsp of salt
- 1 tsp of pepper
- ¼ cup olive oil
- 2 tbsp. of flour
- 1 tsp of garlic powder
- 1/3 cup of diced onions
- ½ tsp of chopped rosemary
- 1 ½ cup of chicken broth

"My sister loved pork chops. Every time I would go to her house, you better believe there were pork chops made––fried, baked, stuffed, or smothered, which was my favorite."

DIRECTIONS

- Start by rinsing the porkchops and drying them thoroughly.
- Add a pinch of salt and pepper to the pork chops.
- Place them in a preheated skillet with ¼ cup of olive oil.
- Brown the pork chops on both sides.
- Add 2 tbsp. of flour in your pan.
- Brown the flour like a rue on med/low flame.
- Add the chicken broth w/onions, salt, pepper and garlic powder (constantly stir until thickened)
- Now add pork chops in and cover.
- Let simmer for 6-10 min.
- Sprinkle the rosemary on top (if desired).
- Take out
- Serve over rice or mash potatoes.

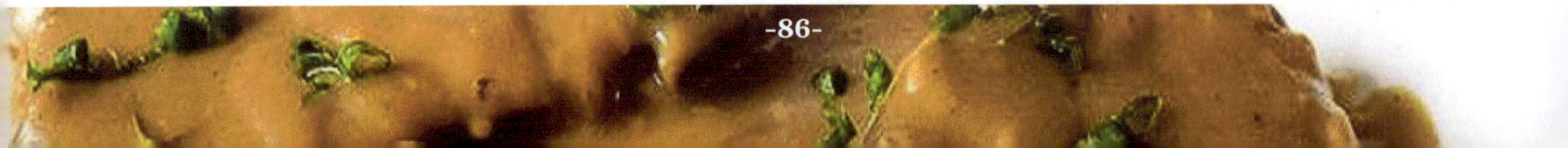

Smothered Pork Chops

My sister loved pork chops. Every time I would go to her house, you better believe there were pork chops made––fried, baked, stuffed, or smothered, which was my favorite. When smothered, the pork chops were topped with onions, seasoning, and oh, let's not forget her special gravy. The gravy was so good that we put it on everything from the rice to the dressing. My sister always believed her pork chops were better than our mother's. They weren't, but I let her believe they were.

Today, when I prepare smothered pork chops, I make plenty so my children and grandchildren can come over and enjoy them. My brother, who didn't eat pork chops, would preach about them not being good for you and that they gave you high blood pressure. But, one night after our family gathering, I remember walking into the kitchen, and guess what I saw? My brother eating pork chops! When I noticed his plate filled with not one but two pork chops, rice, and dressing, I asked him, "How's your blood pressure?" We both just laughed hysterically. I love dinner with my family.

We have the best times. Look at God!

My Notes:

Baked Salmon

INGREDIENTS

- 5 or 6 pieces of Salmon
- ½ cup olive oil or vegetable oil
- 1 onion
- 1 green bell pepper sliced
- 1 tbsp. accent seasoning
- 1 tbsp. fish seasoning
- Pinch of salt
- 1 tbsp. black pepper
- ¼ cup of lemon juice
- Paprika

DIRECTIONS

- Put your salmon in a baking dish with 1/2 cup of oil (of your choice)
- cut the onion into circles to place on top of the salmon along with the sliced green peppers.
- Sprinkle the accent seasoning and fish seasoning with a pinch of salt and black pepper to the salmon.
- Add the lemon juice on top of the salmon
- garnished with a sprinkle of paprika,
- Bake on 350 for 20 minutes.

Baked Salmon

In the past, I've had salmon cooked on the grill with onions and green peppers, which is delicious. However, I decided to shake things up and bake it. Sometimes I mix lime juice with lemon juice, sprinkle it on with some paprika, and wrap it in aluminum foil. I've received several compliments on my baked salmon, which is why I bring it to dinner parties whenever I am invited and have to bring a dish. I was shocked by how many guests never had baked salmon with grilled onions and peppers before but loved mine. They commented on how the different flavors made the fish perfect.

This dish is not only fulfilling, but it tastes amazing and goes perfect with any vegetable. Enjoy!

My Notes:

Squash Casserole

INGREDIENTS

- 4 squashes
- 2 zucchinis
- 1 large onion
- 1 cup of vegetable broth
- 1/3 cup of sour cream
- 2 tbsp. of cornstarch
- 1/2 tsp of garlic powder
- 1/2 cup of shredded sharp cheese
- 2 cups of mild shredded cheese
- 5 slices of pepper jack cheese
- 2 eggs

DIRECTIONS

- Start by cutting the 4 squashed, 2 zucchini and 1 large onion into circles.
- Put all 3 into a large pot.
- Then add 1 cup of vegetable broth.
- Put the top on the pot & let boil for 15min on medium heat.
- Remove and strain.
- Be sure to squeeze out as much liquid as you can out of the squash, using a large spoon with a strainer. (The less liquid the better.)
- Put it in a big bowl.
- Add salt, pepper and a dash of garlic powder.
- Next add the shredded sharp cheese, mild cheese, and 5 slices pepper jack cheese mixed with sour cream, cornstarch and add 2 eggs (already whisked)
- Mix everything together.
- Pour it all into a large casserole dish.
- Bake at 350 degrees for 1 hour or until golden brown.
- Cover the top with mild cheese put back into the oven for 5-10 min
- Take out and cool for 10-15 min.
- Eat and Enjoy.

Please note that this dish can be made with vegetarian cheese (if desired)

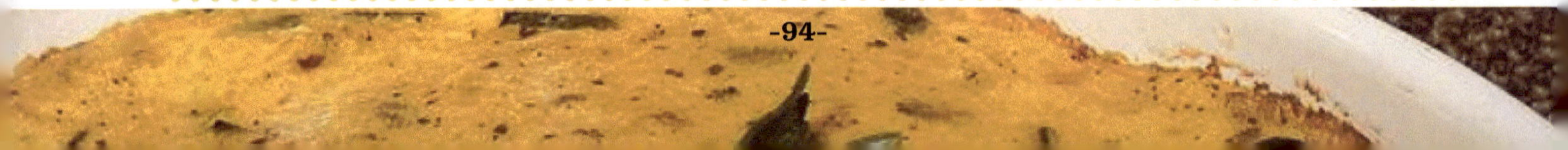

Squash Casserole

This dish was my mother's recipe, but I enhanced it. My mom would peel the squash and then add onions and zucchini while frying it––the same as how I make mine. The only thing that I do differently is steam my squash, add cheese, and bake it for about an hour.

Squash casserole is a traditional dish with my family. I had a niece who hated squash casserole, but I would make her eat it. I thought vegetables would keep her healthy. I was raised to believe vegetables are good for the brain and bones and staving off diseases and certain viruses. I still believe that today. However, I am more aware that our digestive systems are different, and we all react differently to foods. At times, I feel bad for making her eat something she hated. So, my precious niece, please forgive me. I did not know then, but I am much better now. LOL!

Three of my children love squash casserole. It was entertaining to watch them fuss over who would get the last of the casserole. To this day, squash casserole is a highly requested dish for family dinners.

I enjoy making the casserole but not as much as I enjoy watching them eat it.

My Notes:

Stuffed Fish

INGREDIENTS

- 1 large trout (or fish of your choice)
- 1 cup of shrimp
- 1/2 tsp of salt
- 1/2 tsp of pepper (sprinkle on fish)
- 1/2 tsp of cayenne pepper
- 1/2 tsp of onion powder
- 1 tbsp. of mustard
- 1 tbsp. of mayonnaise
- 1/2 tsp of minced garlic
- 1 tbsp. of lemon juice
- Fresh parsley (chopped finely)
- 2 cans of lump crab meat
- 1 tbsp of fish seasoning

DIRECTIONS

- Slice your fish down the middle to remove all of the inside (make sure the inside is cleaned)
- Take a paper towel and dry the inside of the fish thoroughly.
- On a baking dish of your choice be sure to spray the dish with oil.
- Place the fish on the dish and sprinkle a little salt and pepper inside the fish.
- In a mixing bowl, add 2 cans of the lump crab meat, shrimp, mustard, mayo, minced garlic, onion powder, Cayenne pepper, parsley flakes, fish seasoning and a pinch of salt and pepper. (Be sure when mixing the crabmeat and shrimp that you fold the meat rather than stirring).
- Take a large spoon to scoop and stuff the mixture of crab meat inside of the fish.
- Make sure to stuff tightly to ensure when you close the fish for baking, that nothing falls out (we want to keep all of the yummy goodness inside)
- Sprinkle a pinch of salt, pepper and the lemon juice on top of the fish
- Bake at 350 degrees for 25-30 min. Take out and serve.

Stuffed Fish

In my hometown, some of the stores sold what they called a Dollar Box, which, like its name, only cost a dollar. The thing with the Dollar Box is it was always filled with different meats, but you never knew what you were getting until you opened the box at home.

One day, we went to the store to buy this dollar box. When we got back home, we found that our box contained a large fish along with shrimp and crab meat. My sisters and I sat in the kitchen watching as our mother prepared the fish. First, she would scale it. Then she cut it down the middle to clean out its insides before seasoning it with salt, pepper, and other spices. Next, she took the crab meat, mixed it with shrimp, and stuffed it inside the fish right before putting it in the oven.

My sisters and I didn't have much patience at our age back then as we sat around waiting to taste our mother's new creation. Like everything else my mother cooked, my siblings and I loved the stuffed fish.

It became a favorite of ours, but we would only get to have it whenever my mom happened to get the Dollar Box filled with seafood.

My Notes:

Stuffed Pork Chops

INGREDIENTS

- 3-4 thick pork chops
- 1 box of cornbread stuffing
- 1 tsp Salt
- 1 tsp Pepper

"My sister, Earthalean, had her special recipe for making pork chops that she would not share with anybody."

DIRECTIONS

- Use 1 box of cornbread stuffing, follow the directions on the box.
- After thoroughly washing your 3 inch or thicker pork chops.
- Cut a long split into them.
- Let the dressing cool off before stuffing the pork chops tightly with finished dressing. Use a pinch of salt and pepper on top of pork chops.
- Use toothpicks along the front to hold in the stuffing.
- Bake for 45 min at 350 degrees.
- Take out and let it rest for 5 mins.
- Best served with yams or baked sweet potatoes.

Stuffed Pork Chops

My sister, Earthalean, had her special recipe for making pork chops that she would not share with anybody. Earthalean would get the thickest pork chops I've ever seen, split them in half, stuff them with her homemade dressing, and then top them off with gravy. Those pork chops were so big that before putting them in the oven, she would stick toothpicks in them to ensure they were tightly closed and no stuffing came out.

While those juicy pork chops baked, I remember thinking to myself, Earthalean, you need to stop talking and go check on those pork chops to make sure they don't burn or dry out. Whenever food was cooking, you could always find my sister engaged in somebody's conversation. As much as I wanted to say something, I would remain quiet because I knew she was a pro at cooking. Plus, her pork chops always came out delicious. So, I trusted that Earthalean knew what she was doing.

You may be wondering where the name Earthalean came from? Well, my mother had two sets of twins that did not live. One day, my grandmother told my mom that she had a dream that if she named my sister after the earth, then she would live. So, my mother did just that and named my sister Earthalean.

**My sister was always different,
even her cooking.**

My Notes:

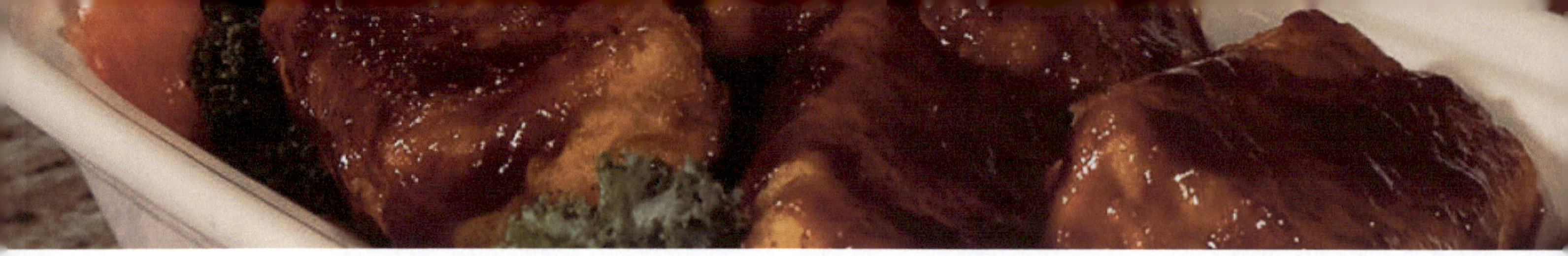

Fried BBQ Tofu

INGREDIENTS

- 1 pack of firm Tofu
- ⅓ tbsp onion powder
- 1 tsp salt
- 1 tsp pepper
- 1 tsp cinnamon
- 1 tbsp. minced garlic
- vegetable oil
- BBQ sauce
- Flour
- 1 egg

DIRECTIONS

- You want to start by draining your tofu on a napkin of some kind. (I've found wrapping it in a tea towel and allowing it to sit for at least ½ hour helps drain most of the water)
- Be sure it is well drained before prepping.
- Season the tofu with a sprinkle of salt, pepper, cinnamon, onion powder and minced garlic (season it to your taste).
- Keep in mind tofu takes on the taste of whatever it is mixed with.
- Season the flour with salt and pepper.
- Whisk an egg
- dip tofu in the egg first, then in the flour, then dip it back into the egg and flour once more (you should have dipped the tofu in the batter and flour twice).
- In a pot filled halfway with oil, on a medium flame, Make sure your oil is HOT before dropping into the oil
- Cook tofu until golden brown.
- Take it out and Drain on a paper towel.
- DRIZZLE BBQ over the top.

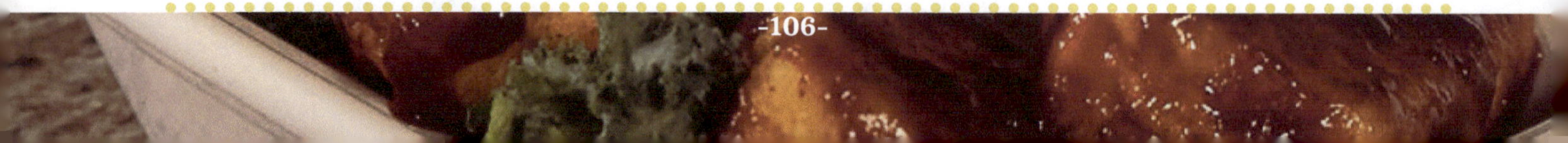

Fried BBQ Tofu

A good friend of mine asked me to cook for an event she was hosting. Even though I've cooked for many parties, this one was an all-vegetarian dinner party with over twenty guests who did not eat any meat. Immediately, I panicked. What would I cook?

"Come on, Evelyn. You can do this. I'm really counting on you. Everything you make is amazing," my friend told me.

With her support, I started my research to learn what vegetarians ate.

While researching, I learned tofu is a dish that vegetarians enjoy. Tofu is a meat replacement made of condensed soy milk, and it takes on the flavor of whatever you prepare with it. It also holds water, so you have to constantly dry it before cooking.

Because it was a backyard summer dinner party, I decided to prepare a BBQ tofu dish that would offer the taste of barbecue chicken. I cut the tofu into flat pieces as if it were chicken breast, mixed up my special barbecue sauce, and poured it on top. Can you say, major hit?! The guests loved it! Some made it into sandwiches, while others ate it with veggies. I still make this dish when my daughters decide they are no longer eating meat.

Whether hosting a party or cooking for a family, this is a perfect dish for all vegetarians.

My Notes:

Quick Cook Spaghetti

"As a mother of six children, having quick meals to cook and serve was a skill set I had to develop, adopt, and master to keep things sane and settled in our home."

INGREDIENTS

- ½ pack of spaghetti noodles
- 1 jar of tomato sauce (of your choice)
- ½ lb. of ground beef
- 1 tsp. of minced garlic
- ½ cup of cherry tomatoes
- ½ cup dice onions
- ½ cup of green peppers
- ½ cup of celery
- 2 tbsp. of olive oil
- Cilantro
- Parsley flakes
- Mozzarella cheese (shredded)
-

DIRECTIONS

- In a skillet add 2 tbsp. of olive oil to a medium heat.
- Add the ½ lb. of ground beef along with your onions, celery, cherry tomatoes, green peppers, minced garlic and garlic powder. As well as a pinch of salt and pepper.
- Mix well. Once the meat is brown
- Add the jar of tomato sauce and add your cilantro
- Turn it down and Let the sauce simmer for 10-15 min.
- While the sauce is simmering, In a separate pot bring your water, 1 tsp of oil and a tsp salt to a boil.
- Then add your noodles. Let it cook for 10 min or until ready.
- Drain the noodles before placing them in a dish of your choice. Add your sauce on top of your noodles.
- Finally sprinkle mozzarella cheese and parsley for your finishing garnish.

Quick Cook Spaghetti

At times, I would refer to myself as "A Quick Cook" simply because I can prepare a whole meal between thirty minutes to an hour. Nowadays, that timeframe may change depending on what I am cooking.

As a mother of six children, having quick meals to cook and serve was a skill set I had to develop, adopt, and master to keep things sane and settled in our home. You see, we typically ate dinner no later than 5:30 p.m. However, having six children with six different after-school activities, dinner time often changed. I did not allow our ever-changing schedule to keep our family from having home-cooked meals daily, though.

So, if you are a working mom or a mom who has many schedules, my quick spaghetti dish takes no time to cook, and your children will enjoy it. I know mine did. I'm sure yours will, as well

My quick spaghetti dish takes no time to cook, and your children will enjoy it!

My Notes:

Fried Mushroom Oysters

"Seafood is a must in my food repertoire, but determining which one is my favorite would require reflecting on Aunt Vee's recipes. "

INGREDIENTS

- 1 pack of oyster mushroom
- 2 cups of flour
- 1 cup of cornmeal
- 2 cups of buttermilk
- 1 tbsp. cajun seasoning
- 1 tsp. salt
- oil

DIRECTIONS

- In a medium size pan, heat your oil on a medium flame.
- Start by pulling apart your oyster mushrooms.
- Then pour buttermilk in a medium size bowl and add the oysters' mushrooms.
- Place cornmeal, flour, Cajun seasoning and salt in a large bowl and whisk to combine
- Take the oysters one at a time from the buttermilk and place in the cornmeal mixture. Toss gently and make sure oysters are coated all over.
- When oil is ready, carefully add the oysters, 5-6 oysters at a time.
- Allow oysters to fry for 2-3 minutes or until golden brown.
- Place cooked oysters on a dry paper towel to drain.
- Repeat until all oysters are cooked.

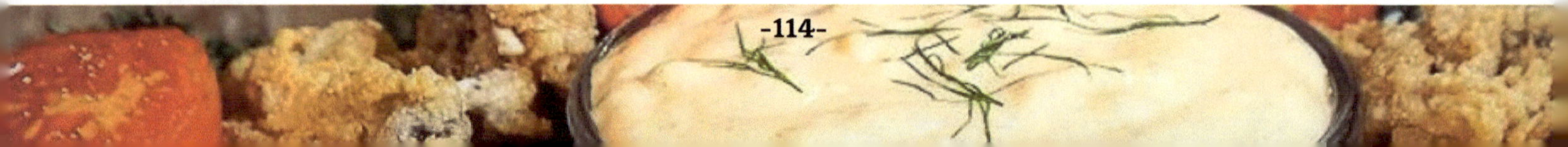

Fried Mushroom Oysters

Seafood is a must in my food repertoire, but determining which one is my favorite would require reflecting on Aunt Vee's recipes. You see, Aunt Vee and I made quite a great team when cooking and creating quick meals. One of my favorite concoctions she created was her fried oysters with a remoulade sauce.

Auntie Vee lived on one of the Sea Islands of South Carolina for many decades. Her cooking is authentically rooted in the Gullah tradition. For those who may not know, Gullah are black people who live on the coast of South Carolina and nearby islands. They are proud of their West African heritage and are diligent in preserving their unique culture. Gullah recipes are based on rice, simmered vegetables, and fresh seafood. Specifically, oysters, shrimp, grits, and okra are commonly incorporated. One of their traditions was feasting on meals and stirring pots with Gullah beenyahs, or natives, at community gatherings, church potlucks, and backyard cookouts. Auntie Vee's meals always remained true to the Gullah tradition. Every dish showcased tasty vegetables and herbs from her great home-grown garden and the freshest seafood from local boat owners and dock workers. She would whip up a Gullah dish anytime you visited––announced or unannounced. In addition to her food, Auntie Vee was famous for her Gullah-inspired homemade wines made from plums, scuppernongs, and blackberries, which my uncle grows in his yard.

Anytime my friends and I were close to her home, we had to stop by, of course. Immediately, my uncle would pull out wine glasses, and we would select the wine. After a few polite sips with the guests, my aunt and I retreated to the kitchen for private time to cook, laugh, and converse. No topics were ever off limits with Auntie Vee! I always have a wonderful time reminiscing, storytelling, and soaking up colorful and cultural tidbits whenever I visit. I always look forward to seeing her because, next to my mother, Auntie Vee is one of the most remarkable women I have ever known.

Now, prepare your palettes for one of the greatest, most delectable Gullah seafood dishes!

My Notes:

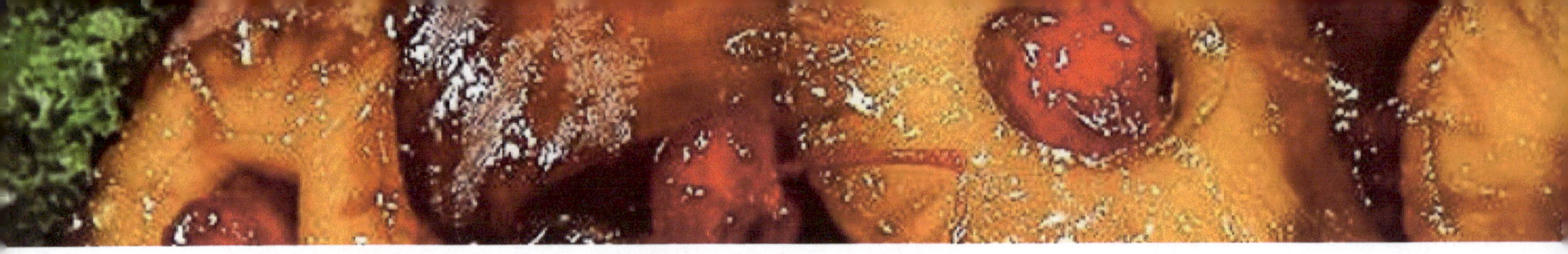

Honey...I'm Hammmmm

INGREDIENTS

- 1 Half Ham (15-20 lbs.)
- 1 Half (½) cup butter or margarine
- 1/3 cup softened butter or margarine
- 1 bottle honey
- 1 box or bag light brown sugar
- 1 can of cherries
- 1 can of circle pineapples
- 1 can cola

DIRECTIONS

- Line the bottom of the pan with 1 cup of brown sugar and ⅓ cup of margarine or softened butter.
- Set aside.
- Rinse ham thoroughly.
- Dry ham off with paper towels.
- Place the ham into the pan (I like to place the fatty part down as opposed to the sliced side. This is optional according to liking).
- Rub the entire exposed portion of ham with 1-cup butter or margarine.
- Squeeze a bottle of honey onto ham (yes it will stick)
- Wash hands. After drying hands, add brown sugar on top of honeyed ham.
- Next take your Pineapples and Cherries to place over your ham. I recommend inserting the cherries in the center of the pineapple and seal them both in place by using a toothpick (be sure to push toothpick in as far as it can go but also leave room enough to grab)
- Finally, pour ½ can of cola into the base of the pan. Do not pour over ham.
- Place in the oven at 300 degrees.
- Baste after 1-½ hours. During this time, you may cover with foil, as the sugar coating begins to melt.
- Continue to bake ham for 20 minutes per pound.The sweet coating tends to char your ham...but this is just sweet honey goodness. Baste ham again every 45 mins. Adding more cola if needed. Using a meat thermometer, remove ham once optimal internal temperature is reached (which is typically 163 degrees in thickest part of ham).

Honey...I'm Hammmmm

One of my fondest memories of the holidays was when my mother would cut the ham in half and place it into two separate pans. Watching her do that always made my siblings and me excited because, in our minds, we were getting TWO HAMS! One day, I asked my mother, "When you bake a ham, why do you cut it in half?"

"I don't know," she told me. "This is the way my mom makes her ham."

Still curious, I went to ask Grandma Katherine.

"Grandma Katherine, my mom said she cuts her ham in half because it's the way you make yours. Why do you cut your ham in half when baking it?" I asked her.

My grandmother responded by saying, "I don't know. I got that from my mother."

Then, still wanting to know, I went to ask my great-grandma Sophie.

"Grandma Sophie, I asked both my mom and grandma why they cut their hams in half when cooking, and they both said they got that from you. Why do you cut your ham in half when baking it?" I asked.

Grandma Sophie's response was priceless.

"I don't know why your mom and grandma do it, but as for me, I could never find a pan big enough to fit the whole thing."

Tradition is something that is passed down from generation to generation. Sometimes we don't know why we do certain things. Most of the time, it's because of what we have seen growing up.

As for me, I will stick with cooking the whole ham in one pan.

My Notes:

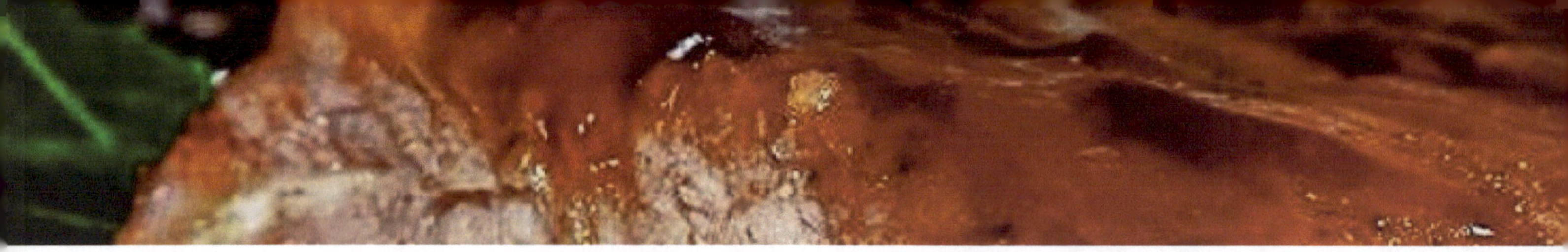

Lauren's Favorite Ribs

INGREDIENTS

- Slab of Ribs
- 1 tsp salt
- 1 tsp pepper
- 1 tsp cayenne pepper
- 1 tbsp. of instant coffee
- 2 tbsp. Lemon juice
- 1 tbsp. of Garlic powder
- 1 tsp of cinnamon
- 2 tbsp. of brown sugar
- 1/2 can of tomato paste
- 1 cup of chicken broth
- 1/4 cup of mustard

DIRECTIONS

- You first want to start off by washing off your slab of ribs and placing them on a pan. Next, you're going to create a rub.
- In a bowl, add your salt, pepper, cayenne pepper and instant coffee, mix it well.
- Then apply the rub onto the ribs, evenly in foil. You want to wrap the ribs up tightly before putting the ribs on the pan, in the oven at 350 degrees.
- Bake for 1hr.

Sauce:

- In a bowl, add a half a can of tomato paste with 1 cup of chicken broth.
- Add your lemon juice, garlic powder, brown sugar, cinnamon and mustard.
- Mix all of the ingredients evenly until the consistency is a little thick (but not too thick). When the ribs are just about done remove the ribs from the oven and carefully spread the sauce onto of the ribs.
- Wrap the ribs back up
- Place them back in the oven to finish cooking for an additional 30 mins or until your desire.

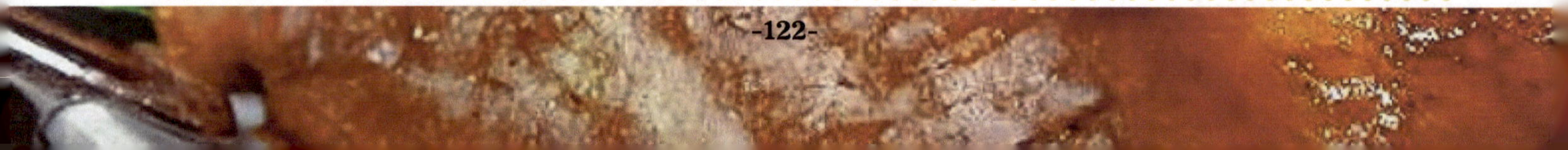

Lauren's Favorite Ribs

When my granddaughter Lauren was a child, she loved watching her aunts and me cook ribs. It did not matter whether they were baked, fried, or grilled, as long as they were ribs.

Her aunt, Traci, who was much like a second mom to her, would make ribs for Lauren just about every other week. Lauren enjoyed her ribs but not as much as she liked to suck on the bones. Whenever someone reminded her that there were more ribs in the kitchen, Lauren would reply, "I know, but I like to suck the bones because they are so sweet"

Lauren had such a bubbly personality and made sure everyone was in a positive, great mood. Because of her spirit, no one ever told her no when she requested her favorite dish.

One Thanksgiving, Lauren secretly asked each of her aunts––Toni, Traci, Towanda, Trina, and Tamar––to make her favorite dish. Lauren came and asked me if I would make her favorite, also, which of course, I agreed to do, not knowing she had already made the same request of my daughters. When we all gathered in the kitchen to start prepping our dishes, it was at that moment we realized we had been bamboozled. When Lauren saw everyone in the kitchen preparing to make the ribs, she belted out the biggest laugh.

I no longer eat ribs as often as I used to because it brings back too many memories of my sweet granddaughter. I think about her often and can still hear her laugh and picture her beautiful smile. Sometimes when I feel sad, I can hear her say, "Mom-Mom, don't be sad. I am here with you." I instantly smile because even though she is no longer here in the flesh, her spirit and energy still live deep within me.

Lauren, you were the light of this family, and your spirit will forever be with us. We love you very much.

My Notes:

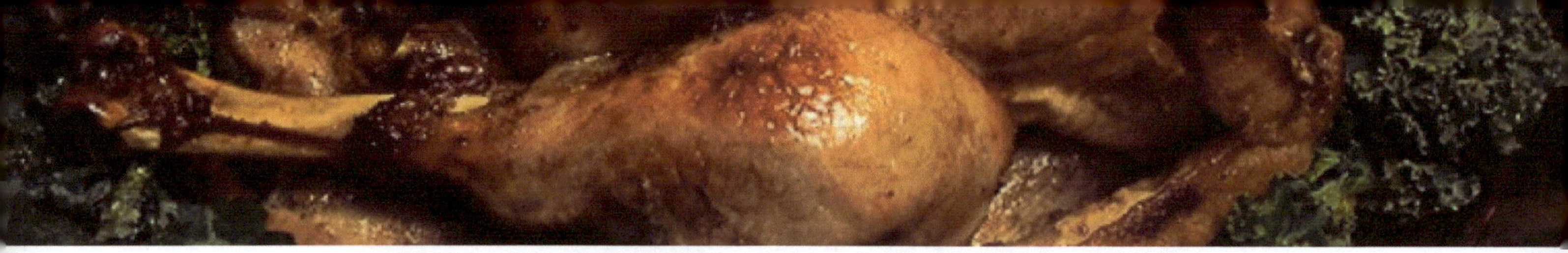

Thanksgiving Turkey

INGREDIENTS

- 15lb Turkey
- ½ stick Butter
- ¼ cup olive oil
- 1 small onion
- 1 tbsp. sage
- 1 tbsp. salt
- 1 tbsp. pepper
- 1 tbsp. poultry seasoning

"Can you feel my excitement?
I truly enjoy preparing and cooking for the Thanksgiving holiday."

DIRECTIONS

- Thaw Turkey overnight.
- Clean your turkey and please don't forget to take the bag from the inside of the turkey. Mix all seasonings together and sprinkle all over the turkey, don't forget the inside.
- Cut the onion in thin circles and place them inside the turkey.
- Place turkey in a roasting pan and bake for ½ hrs. per pound on 325 degrees.
- Turkey should be golden brown. Allow the turkey to rest 10-20mins before carving.

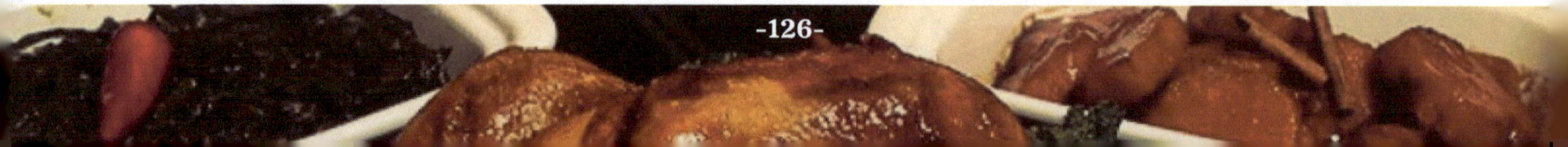

Thanksgiving Turkey

Thanksgiving is a dinner the pilgrims and Indians created, Americans adopted, and which has become a national tradition for many generations. When I think about Thanksgiving, I get excited about all the dishes I will cook––ham, dressing, pies, and especially the turkey. Can you feel my excitement? I truly enjoy preparing and cooking for the Thanksgiving holiday.

I mean, who doesn't like Thanksgiving. The aroma of the food alone makes me happy. The fire that dances in the fireplace and the fellowship between family and friends is priceless. The competition for the best chef title amongst family members is always enjoyable to watch. Then there are those family members who don't bring anything to dinner other than their appetites. Thanksgiving is a time when we all get to enjoy life with those we love. Again, priceless.

Honestly, I don't think the turkey knows how much effect it has on people, especially my children. After having dinner, all of my children would fall asleep, and there would be quiet throughout the house. It never failed. I think I enjoy that part of Thanksgiving the most, especially after cooking all day.

Another thing I love about Thanksgiving is creating meals using the leftovers. Turkey sandwiches were always the best the next day. Now I understand some families don't celebrate Thanksgiving, but allow me to offer my concept. Thanksgiving is not about the food; it is solely rooted in fellowship and family. Yes, Thanksgiving and its birth may have a negative and evil connection to it, but we cannot forget what the moment stood for prior.

I am not making light of the violence but instead remembering the joy and spirit of the true intent of the Native Americans and what they stand for.

We have to always look for value and peace in order to honor our past.

My Notes:

Ms. E's Words of Wisdom:

"We have to always look for value and peace in order to honor our past."

Ms E's
BRAXTON
Recipes
~Side Dishes~

Fried Cabbage

INGREDIENTS

- 1 small cabbage
- 2 tbsp of olive oil
- 1 medium size onion
- ½ of red onion
- 1/2 tsp. of salt
- 1/2 tbsp of cracked pepper
- 1/2 tsp. of sage
- 2 tbsp. of chicken broth
- 1 green pepper

"Due to my father being a diabetic, sweet treats were only allowed on special occasions. So, one of our favorite after-school snacks was sweet potatoes and fried cabbage."

DIRECTIONS

- Wash your cabbage head.
- Cut your cabbage into 4 different parts
- Then recut the parts into very small and thin portions.
- Cut your onions and green pepper.
- Into a medium size pot add 2 tbsp olive oil and your diced onions and green peppers. Let them sauté over medium/high heat.
- Place your cabbage into your pot and add the rest of your ingredients.
- Turn your pot on medium/low heat.
- Consistently stir for 20 minutes.
- Note: This dish makes a great side for baked chicken, stuffed chicken, and a full course meal.

Fried Cabbage

Every day, my sisters and I would come home from school wanting a snack. Due to my father being a diabetic, sweet treats were only allowed on special occasions. So, one of our favorite after-school snacks was sweet potatoes and fried cabbage.

You see, we lived within the city limits of a South Carolina town and had what we called a "vegetable and fruit man." He would come to our house every day selling fruits and vegetables that were "organic." This was convenient because my parents never had to go to the market––at least not for fruits and vegetables.

Even though my mother didn't prepare fried cabbage every day, it would literally make our little mouths water when she did.

My Notes:

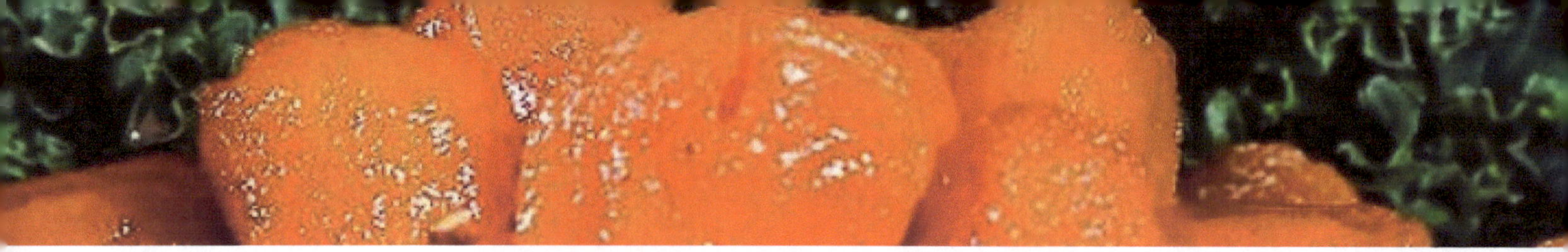

Glazed Carrots

"Knowing how much I disliked carrots, my mother came up with a creative way to get me to eat them."

INGREDIENTS

- 5 fresh carrots
- 1 tbsp. of butter
- 1/3 cups of brown sugar
- 1 tbsp. of vanilla extract
- 1 cup of water
- Pinch of salt
- Pinch of pepper
- 1/2 tsp of cinnamon
- 2 tbsp. of syrup

DIRECTIONS

- Cut your carrots into small chunky pieces.
- In a medium sized pan, add all of your ingredients.
- Cover your pan and let simmer on medium/high heat for 20-30 minutes until fork tender.
- Consistently stir carrots, cook water down until it starts to glaze.
- Add your syrup
- after the carrots have glazed, let cook slowly for about 5 more minutes.
- This dish is quick, fast, tasty and healthy. Enjoy!

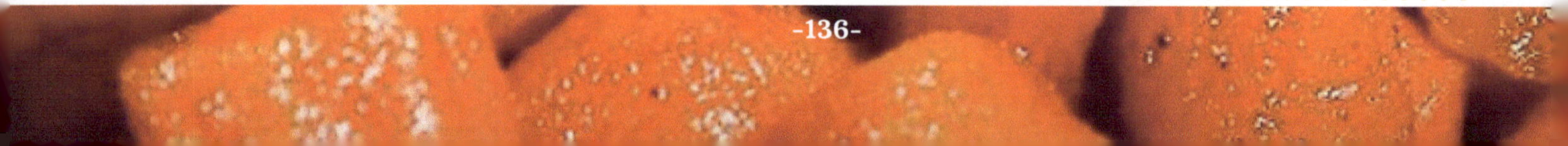

Glazed Carrots

Knowing how much I disliked carrots, my mother came up with a creative way to get me to eat them. She would put a sweet glaze on them, which quickly converted my dislike of carrots to loving them. She always said, "Carrots will make you have pretty eyes."
I thought if I ate enough of them, my eyes would become light brown like my sisters'. So, wanting light brown eyes, I began eating more and more. Unfortunately, it didn't work; my eye color remained dark brown! Then I learned that they help improve your eyesight, and, for me, that was good enough.

**If your carrots taste like carrots after making this recipe,
you did something wrong. They should remind you of candied yams.**

My Notes:

Grilled Asparagus

INGREDIENTS

- 1 bunch of asparagus
- 1 chicken breast
- 1 lemon
- ¼ cup of olive oil
- 1 tbsp. of black pepper
- 1 tsp of salt
- 1 tbsp. ground rosemary
- 1 tsp poultry seasoning
- 1 tsp Sage
- 1 tbsp. of garlic powder
- Meat cleaver
- Saran Wrap
- Parchment paper

DIRECTIONS

- Take the chicken breast and cut it into thin pieces the long way.
- Season the chicken with garlic powder, rosemary, salt, sage, poultry season, and black pepper.
- On a flat surface, lay some saran wrap to place the chicken.
- With a meat cleaver, tenderize the chicken as thin as you can get it.
- Wash the asparagus and trim the ends off.
- In a bowl, squeeze the lemon over the asparagus.
- Add the olive oil, a pinch of black pepper, garlic powder and salt, mix ingredients together.

(The wrapping)

- Take a thin slice of chicken breast and place it on the parchment paper.
- Take the asparagus and starting from the bottom wrap the chicken around gradually going upward.
- Place wrapped asparagus in a skillet with medium heat.
- Add 1 tablespoon of olive oil.
- Cook for 5 minutes on each side until golden.

Grilled Asparagus

Asparagus was a dish my family did not eat frequently; it was always a surprise or special occasion when we did. Over time, I acquired a taste for this dish. When my mother added lemon to them, it changed the taste, and I gained a true love for this dish. Whenever she would fix them, I would get excited because I knew the asparagus would be tantalizing to my taste buds. My children ate asparagus as a snack after school, but I believe they liked the idea of them being a stick. Enjoy!

Ring the joy and spirit of the true intent of the Native Americans and what they stand for.

My Notes:

Kale

INGREDIENTS

- 3 bunched of kale (cut into small pieces)
- 1 medium size onion
- 1 tsp. of poultry seasoning
- 1 tsp. of sage
- 2 bay leaves
- 1 tbsp of brown sugar
- 2 cups of vegetable broth
- ½ tsp. of salt
- 3 tbsp. of pepper
- ¼ cup of olive oil

"Kale is an attractive plant that reminds me of a flower, and it is good for you"

DIRECTIONS

- Wash kale very thoroughly to rid of all sand and debris.
- Sauté onions until they start to brown.
- Meanwhile, strip your kale from the stem.
- Add kale to the pot with 2 cups of vegetable broth, bay leaves and brown sugar
- Put a top on the pot.
- Stir and fold over frequently, over medium heat for about an hour or tender.

Kale

I was born in the South; however, I grew up in Maryland. My aunt Juanita adopted me at an early age, and the life I knew in the South slowly changed after I was introduced to new and different foods––kale being one of them.

She and Uncle Roland ate kale for lunch and dinner every day. I swear it seemed like she had the largest pot in the world and would prepare enough kale that would last about three to four days. When I tell you, we had kale in every way imaginable. Raw, cooked, baked––you name it! My aunt would also use kale as a garnish.

Kale is an attractive plant that reminds me of a flower, and it is good for you. But, when preparing kale, make sure you rip the leaves from the stem and wash them thoroughly. There is nothing worse than eating gritty kale!

There is nothing worse than eating gritty kale!

My Notes:

Ms. E's Collard Greens

INGREDIENTS

- 3 bunch of collard greens
- 1 small pack of smoked turkey parts
- 2 cups of chicken broth
- 2-3 Bay leaves
- 1 tsp of brown sugar
- pinch of baking soda
- 2 tbsp. of olive oil
- 1 cup of chopped onions
- 3 tbsp. of salt
- 3 tbsp. of pepper

"Collard greens will always hold a special place in my heart because of the memories I made while cooking them with my mother."

DIRECTIONS

- Sauté the onions in the olive oil over medium heat.
- Pour chicken broth into the pot.
- Add greens, bay leaves, smoked turkey, salt and pepper
- Then add Brown sugar and baking soda.
- Stir and fold over frequently, over a medium heat for about an hour or tender.

Ms. E's Collard Greens

Collard greens were an all-time favorite of mine. Often, I would help my mother prepare collard greens by washing them, rolling them, and then cutting them very thin. My mom would have a fit if they were too thick. She also loved to eat the stem. But, now, I cut the leaves from the stem when I prepare them. To me, they cook a lot quicker that way.

Collard greens will always hold a special place in my heart because of the memories I made while cooking them with my mother.

That's probably why I'm a better cook than my siblings, but don't tell them I said that. LOL!

My Notes:

Ms. E's Macaroni & Cheese

INGREDIENTS

- 1 box of macaroni noodles
- 2 cups of Milk
- 1 tsp. of pepper
- 1 tsp. of salt
- 1 cup of sour cream
- 1 tsp of mustard
- 1 pack of American sliced cheese
- 1 pack of Mozzarella Cheese
- 1 pack of mild cheese
- 1 pack of sharp cheese
- 1 pack of pepper jack cheese

DIRECTIONS

- Preheat the oven to 350 degrees.
- In a medium pot Add water, salt and 1 tbsp. of olive oil.
- Bring the water to a boil then add noodles.
- Allow noodles to boil for 30 minutes or until tender.
- Drain noodles. Then Pour noodles into a large bowl
- In a pot on a low flame, add your sour cream and milk, whisk well.
- Then add the pepper, mustard and all of your cheese.
- Mix all ingredients together. Let everything melt together until it becomes a thick sauce.
- Next add your noodles to the pot and stir everything together.
- Finally pour your macaroni into a casserole dish.
- Bake for 1 hour.
- Remove from the oven and add a layer of mild cheese on the top.
- Put back into the oven for 10 more minutes.
- Remove from the oven and let cool.
- Enjoy!

Ms. E's Macaroni & Cheese

When it came to preparing side dishes, my mom usually only prepared rice or potatoes. I guess you can say that's a Geechee thing. In the south, specifically South Carolina, they ate rice or potatoes with everything. For some, it is considered a main dish. Mom rarely made macaroni and cheese, and I am not sure why. Maybe it was because it wasn't my father's favorite, or perhaps she didn't particularly care for it either.

However, when she did make macaroni and cheese, it was a special treat. I remember it melting in my mouth as a kid.

Even though we didn't have it often, it somehow became one of my and my siblings' favorite meals.

My Notes:

Cheesy Fried Rice

"We ate rice with every meal, it was one leftover we had quite often."

INGREDIENTS

- 2 cups of cooked Rice (or you can use left over rice, if it's not mushy)
- 1tsp Salt
- 1 tsp Pepper
- 1/4 cup of olive oil
- 1 ½ tsp. Garlic powder
- 1tsp. sage
- 1 tsp. poultry seasoning
- 1 tbsp. onion powder (season to your preference)
- 1/2 cup of sharp cheese
- 1 cup of pepper jack cheese
- 1/4 cup of chicken broth

DIRECTIONS

- In the pan add olive oil, and a pinch of salt & pepper.
- To your liking add the garlic powder, sage, poultry seasoning & onion powder.
- Next add sharp cheese, pepper jack cheese and chicken broth.
- Mix together and pour over the rice.
- Stir together for 3 to 5 mins.
- Pour your rice into a casserole dish.
- Bake at 350 degrees for 15-20 minutes.
- Take it out of the oven, allow it to cool and serve.

Cheesy Fried Rice

Growing up in a home with multiple brothers and sisters, having leftovers were very common because my mother always fixed plenty of food. Since we ate rice with every meal, it was one leftover we had quite often. There were times my siblings and I would get so tired of eating rice that we dreaded the sight of it. But, when I was a kid, you gratefully ate what was placed in front of you. My mom did not want to hear, nor did she care about, what you didn't like unless you were allergic to it.

One day, my mother realized just how much my siblings and I were tired of eating rice. I mean, we were over it! However, instead of her making another dish, she surprised us by preparing the rice differently. She added cheese and then placed it in a skillet with oil as if she was going to fry the rice. Wait, no pot? At that point, I was utterly confused about what she was doing. I loved to watch my mom cook because she made it look easy and enjoyable, but I was stumped with her use of a skillet while cooking the rice. Later I learned she was making cheesy fried rice. As I watched her prepare it, I became excited to taste it because it looked and smelled great. And boy was it!

My siblings and I loved it so much that we wanted cheesy fried rice every day forward. The regular white or brown rice was played out to us. I still love cheesy fried rice today. I've since discovered that baking it tastes just as good as eating it straight out of the pan like my mother used to make it.

Today, I make it for my grandbabies, and they love it, too. Look at God!

My Notes:

Rice Pudding

INGREDIENTS

- 2 cups of cooked rice (of leftover rice)
- 3 eggs (whisk)
- 1 tbsp. vanilla Flavor
- 1 cup of half & half
- ½ cup of milk
- 1 cup & ½ of sugar
- 1 tbsp. of cinnamon
- ½ tbsp. of nutmeg
- 1 cup of raisins

"Honestly, I think
Aunt Juanita lived just to make rice pudding..."

DIRECTIONS

- First boil your 2 cups of rice until done and let it cool, (or you can use rice that is left over)
- In a bowl whisk 3 eggs, Vanilla Flavor, half & half, milk, sugar, cinnamon, nutmeg and raisins.
- Then add your cooled rice.
- Mix everything together well.
- Pour your rice in a casserole dish.
- Bake at 350 degrees for 1 hour -1hr 20min or until all dried out.
- Take out and let it cool off for 10 mins.
- Serve

Rice Pudding

While living with my aunt Juanita, I realized she shared the same sentiments regarding leftovers as my mother. She would take any leftover rice and make rice pudding. Honestly, I think she lived just to make rice pudding, as it always put the biggest smile on her face. She would make so much that I would think to myself, Who in the name of God is going to eat all of that? Because Aunt Juanita had gone through so much in life, cooking became therapy for her.

During the time I lived with her, my aunt was in an abusive marriage. It was the saddest thing because no matter how hard she tried to please her husband, her efforts were always met with adversity and negativity. She would bend over forward and backwards for him, but it didn't change how he acted towards her. For instance, when he came home one day, she greeted him by saying, "Good evening." Instead of matching her greeting with love, he replied, "What the hell is good about it?" I also remember her dressing up for him but only being met with body shaming and harsh words. She fought hard to receive his validation, but it was all for naught.

My aunt knew her husband loved rice pudding. Despite all of his negativity towards her, she continued making the tasty dessert for him. She wanted nothing more than to make him happy. Having witnessed all that my aunt with through with her husband, I think it's why I have such a heart for women who suffer from abuse––whether verbally, physically, or mentally.

Such a beautiful lady with such a horrible life. If no one else loved her in that house, I know I did. This is for you, Auntie Nita.

My Notes:

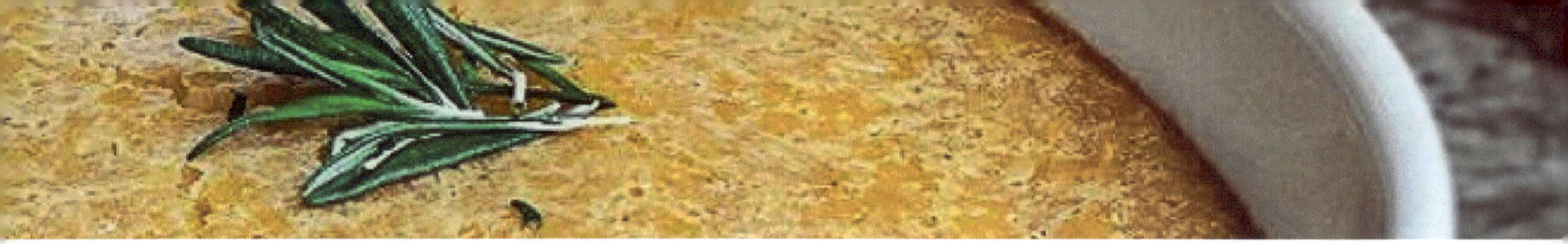

Corn Pudding

INGREDIENTS

- 2 tbsp. All Purpose Flour
- 1-½ stick salted butter
- 1 cup half and half
- 1-cup heavy whipping cream
- ½ cup white sugar
- 1-cup light brown sugar
- 1 tbsp. vanilla flavoring
- 1 tsp. cinnamon
- 2 cans creamed corn
- 2 bags of frozen sweet corn
- 1 large egg.

"I tasted it for myself, and sure enough, it was corn! It was one of the tastiest things I had ever eaten!"

DIRECTIONS

- In a large saucepan, add flour and butter to form a rue (paste).
- Do not brown.
- Add half and half and heavy whipping cream. Stir but do not whisk.
- After ingredients have incorporated, add sugars, flavoring and cinnamon.
- Add creamed corn. Stir and then remove from heat.
- Add frozen corn and stir until fully coated.
- Beat one large egg into the mixture.
- Pour into a greased pan.
- Bake covered at 350 for one hour and 15 mins.
- Let it cool and serve.

Corn Pudding

My children were never huge fans of corn, especially if it wasn't served on the cob. One day, while at a church function, one of the mothers served up a pudding-style dish. All of the young people seemed to flock to that particular bowl. Some even came back for seconds. I was thinking they were substituting their meals for dessert. I even scolded one of my children.

"But, Mommy, it's corn, and it's SWEET!" she told me.

I tasted it for myself, and sure enough, it was corn! My goodness! It was one of the tastiest things I had ever eaten—–unlike anything I had ever experienced.

After asking the young mother for the recipe, it has become a staple in our home, but with my spin on it, of course.

My Notes:

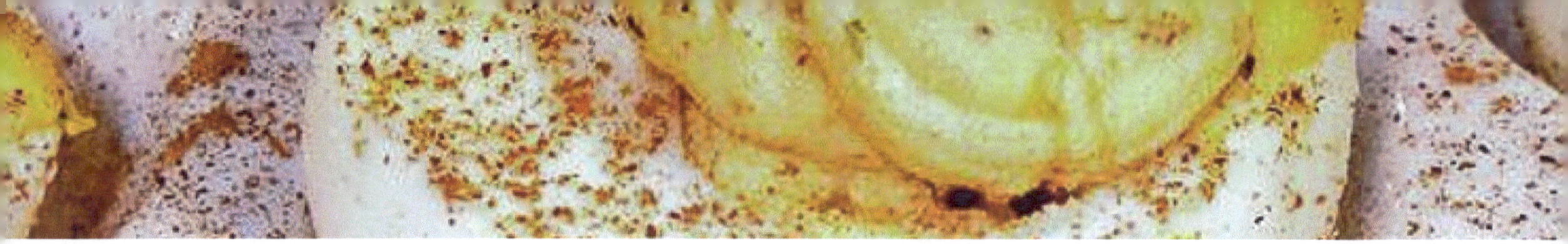

Deviled Eggs

INGREDIENTS

- 1 dozen of Eggs
- ½ tsp of salt
- ½ tsp of pepper
- 1 cup of Mayo
- ½ cup relish
- 1 tbsp. of mustard
- paprika

"Most holidays, events, and private parties were held at my home, and deviled eggs were always a must-have requested by family and guests."

DIRECTIONS

- **Begin by boiling your dozens of eggs in a large boiler for about 15mins.**
- **Let them the cool off before peeling.**
- **Once cooled and peeled, cut each egg in half and with a spoon scoop out the insides of the egg and put the inside in a small mixing bowl.**
- **Then mix in a pinch of salt and pepper along with your mayo, relish and mustard.**
- **Mix everything evenly before adding the mixture to an icing bag or a zip lock bag, this will help you fill each egg nice and neat.**
- **Sprinkle paprika on the top for garnish and a splash of color.**

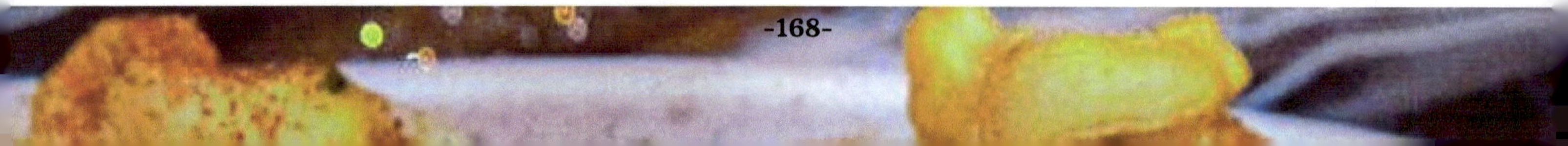

Deviled Eggs

Most holidays, events, and private parties were held at my home, and deviled eggs were always a must-have requested by family and guests. They would always comment how they were so addictive, and they could never eat just one. People would have two or three of them on their plates, especially at my BBQs. My deviled eggs would be gone before the meat could even get done.

"What is your special ingredient that makes your deviled eggs taste so much better than anyone else's?" my sister would ask me.

Smiling, I would reply, "Nothing but love and passion."

I failed to share with her that I added extra relish and sprinkles of paprika. But shhh! Let's wait until she reads the recipe in the book.

My Notes:

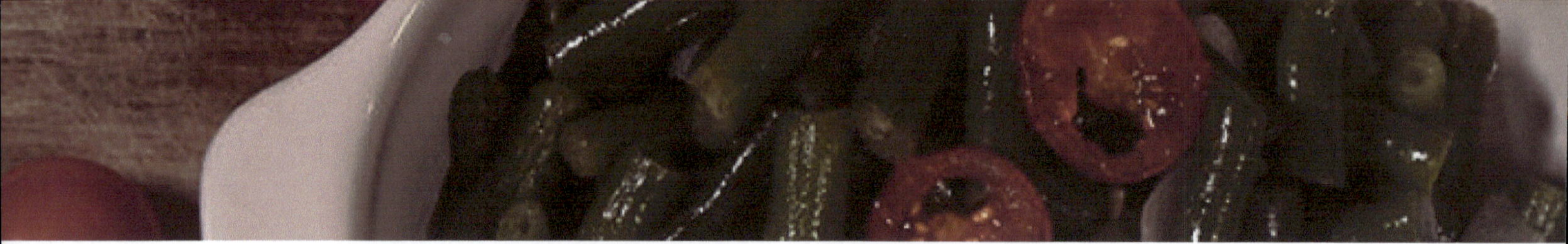

String Beans

INGREDIENTS

- ¼ cup of onions
- 1 cup of string beans
- ½ cup chicken broth (or vegetable broth)
- 1 ½ tbsp. of olive oil
- 1 tsp. of Salt
- 1 tsp. of pepper

"My mom was like the string bean perfectionist; she could tell if we hadn't stripped the string beans the way she had taught us."

DIRECTIONS

- Start by dicing your onion.
- In a pot over medium/high heat, add washed string beans, diced onions, and chicken or vegetable broth.
- Then add olive oil with a pinch of salt and pepper.
- COOK UNTIL TENDER.
- STIR and SERVE.

String Beans

When I was a little girl, I remember my mother sitting on the porch snapping string beans all day long, which was fine with me. The problem came when she would make us snap them, too. And let's be clear, we didn't just snap the beans. We also made sure to remove the string before my mother washed and cooked them. My mom was like the string bean perfectionist; she could tell if we hadn't stripped the string beans the way she had taught us. How did she know? If the string beans were chewy while eating them, that meant we hadn't thoroughly removed the strings, and therefore, they would have to be thrown away. Needless to say, we learned early on the correct way to strip string beans since throwing them away was not an option we wanted to face.

In my opinion, my mother made the best string beans in the world. When she added turkey parts and white potatoes, it gave them an extra special taste. Bon appétit!

My Notes:

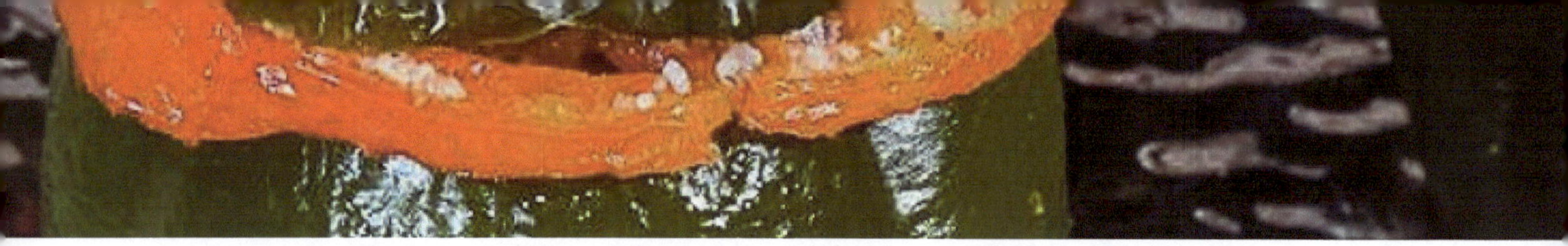

Stuffed Green Peppers

INGREDIENTS

- 4 green peppers
- Ground beef (or ground turkey or chicken) meat of your choice
- ¼ tsp salt
- ¼ tsp pepper
- 1 pack cherry tomatoes (cut in half)
- ½ cup of diced onions (pre- cook)
- 3 cloves of garlic
- Fresh parsley
- 1 tbsp. cilantro
- Pepper jack or Cheese (of your choice)
- Rice (leftover rice work just as well)

DIRECTIONS

- After you have rinsed off your peppers, you want to cut off the top of the peppers to remove the seeds from inside.
- Take your leftover rice, pre-cooked diced onions, cilantro, cherry tomatoes (cut in half), garlic, and parsley in a med size skillet and mix well.
- Add a pinch of salt and pepper as well as Italian seasoning to the mix.
- Next you add the pepper jack (or cheese of your preference) and stir that evenly into the mix.
- Carefully stuff the pepper (fully) with the rice mix.
- You can also add a slice of tomato (season to your liking) on top before placing the top half of the pepper back on.
- Place the stuffed peppers on a cookie sheet, sprayed with a little oil.
- You want to put a pan filled with about 2 cups of water, at the very bottom of your oven. This will allow steam from the water pan to help cook the peppers.
- That should be placed on a rack centered and above the water pan.
- Bake on 350degrees for about an hour or until it is nice and tender.
- When ready, serve with any vegetable of your choice.

*Note: this dish can be prepared for Vegans. (Substitute the ground beef for vegan meat of your choice and use vegan cheese)

Stuffed Green Peppers

My baby sister, Deloris, affectionately known as Lois, loves stuffed green peppers. Whenever I would visit my sister, I knew stuffed green peppers would be served. My sister is what you would call a creature of habit as she would make the same meal each time.

I recall when she had me over for dinner, and, as always, stuffed peppers were on the menu. The aroma in the house smelled so good, and I could hardly wait to eat, especially after seeing how nice and stuffed those peppers looked on Lois's plate.

After taking my first bite, I paused and slowly turned to look at Lois.

"Um, Lois, is that a bean I taste?" I asked.

"Girl, yeah!" she replied. "You know me. I'll use whatever I have leftover. Rice, beans, corn, carrots——you name it. If it's in there, I will use it."

We burst into laughter because we both knew how true that statement was. As my mother would always tell us, "Every food has value. There are people in this world who are hungry, so value the food you do have." Lois took that to heart. Nevertheless, the combination of rice and beans was incredible. Lois would come up with the strangest recipes, and they would be a hit.

Many years ago, Lois became ill and was diagnosed with a herniated disk. My sister would often talk about her arms, legs, and her back hurting. I would sit and watch her in excruciating pain, feeling helpless because there was nothing, I could do nothing to help her aside from praying that she would get some relief. However, despite the pain she experienced, she did not allow it to stop her from making her favorite dishes for the family.

After much convincing, she decided to have her herniated disk fixed. However, we became very concerned after the operation because the doctors conveyed, she may not make it. But then God intervened, and the results changed to her becoming an ambulant. Even though that was not what we wanted to hear either, we were happy she would still be here with us.

Lois is now confined to a wheelchair, unable to walk as she once could. However, her steadfast faith and optimistic attitude keep her strongly believing that one day she will. As Lois adjusted to her new reality, the wheelchair did not stop her love for cooking and creating all her favorite dishes, including her stuffed green peppers. After all these years, she still makes them the same way.

"Whether I walk again or not doesn't matter. The fact that I BELIEVE I WILL WALK AGAIN is all that matters," she always says.

Today, Lois continues to enjoy life——making her favorite meals and inviting me over for dinner. I love my sister beyond measure, and there is nothing I would not do for her. However, if I eat one more stuffed green pepper, I just might turn into one myself!

My Notes:

Red Sauerkraut

INGREDIENTS

- 1 pack of sauerkraut
- ½ tsp of salt
- ½ tsp of pepper
- 1/4 cup of olive oil or avocado oil
- 1/4 cup of ketchup
- 2 cups of chicken broth
- Cut sausage links of your choice (optional)

"I often tell people when they think of sauerkraut to think of life."

DIRECTIONS

- Start by straining and slightly rinsing the 1 pack of sauerkraut.
- In a med pot add the rinsed sauerkraut, ½ onion (diced), salt, pepper, oil of your choice, ketchup and chicken broth.
- Let it simmer on a medium/low heat for about an hour & half.
- *OPTIONAL* you can add all or ½ of the slice sausage link.

Red Sauerkraut

Red sauerkraut is a dish I always enjoyed during Thanksgiving dinner. One of my family members made sauerkraut religiously every year. To me, she made the best sauerkraut you ever wanted to taste. My children loved it just as much as I did, and we all could not wait until the following year to get our hands on more of it.

Then, I was taught how to make it, and from that moment on, the game changed. I immediately taught my children so we could all enjoy the recipe together or separately. Her red sauerkraut always made you feel as if you were eating something exotic. It was always the topic of discussion whenever others would taste it.

The flavor of sauerkraut can be slightly bitter, but it becomes bittersweet if you add a little ketchup and brown sugar. I often tell people when they think of sauerkraut to think of life.

Like sauerkraut, life can be a little complex; it all depends on you and what you add to it.

My Notes:

~DESSERTS~

Ms. E's Words of Wisdom:

"Each generation needs to embrace life and remember the sacrifices our ancestors made to be free and stay free."

Bread Pudding

"Wasting food was a no-no. So, I came up with an idea for the bread that would not only make me happy but make them happy, as well."

INGREDIENTS

- Leftover bread
- 3 Eggs
- 2 apples (diced)
- ½ stick of butter
- 1 tsp of vanilla flavor
- 1 tbsp of rum flavor
- 1 tsp. of Allspice
- 1 cup of sugar
- 1 tbsp. of cinnamon
- 1 cup of Milk (whole milk)
- ½ cup of raisins

DIRECTIONS

- Start by crumpling up any leftover bread you have into a bowl (I usually use my biscuits.)
- Dice up 2 apples to add to the bread crumbles.
- In a mixer bowl. Add eggs, 1/2 stick of butter, and vanilla flavor. If you want a rum flavor, you can add 1 tbsp of rum flavor.
- Then Add "All Spice", cinnamon, sugar (if there is a lot of bread) If not 1/2 cup of sugar will work just fine and MILK (WHOLE MILK).
- Pour liquid mixture into a med size pot on a med flame and stir often.
- Cook it until it's like pudding.
- Then add Raisins in the mixer.
- Mix in your bread crumbles and mix everything together.
- Pour mixture into a medium size casserole dish.
- Place in the oven to bake for 45 min.

Bread Pudding

I would always prepare a meal that included some type of bread for a starter. My children enjoyed yeast rolls, so I made them twice a week. By the end of the week, there would be rolls leftover. Of course, wasting food was a no-no. So, I came up with an idea for the bread that would not only make me happy but make them happy, as well. I decided to use the leftover rolls to make bread pudding!

It was a total success and became a favorite dessert in my home.

Each time, I would make it different––using fruits, nuts, or raisins. Today, bread pudding is a holiday favorite for my family!

My Notes:

Freedom Pie

"Freedom pie is a family tradition passed down from my great-grandmother. My great-grandmother taught my grandmother, who taught my mother, who taught my sisters and me."

INGREDIENTS

- 3 whole medium white potatoes
- ½ stick butter
- 2 cups of brown sugar
- 1tsp salt
- 2 tbsp. of vanilla flavoring
- 2 tbsp. of cinnamon
- 1 tsp. of nutmeg
- 4 eggs
- 2 deep dishes, 9-inch pie crusts (optional)
- ¼ cup of raisins
- ⅓ cup of crushed nuts or pecans (optional)
- 3 tbsp of drained crushed pineapples (optional)

DIRECTIONS

- Peel and cut potatoes into chunks.
- Boil potatoes for 35-40 min or until soft.
- Strain them and put them in a large mixing bowl to mash.
- Then add your butter, brown sugar, Vanilla flavoring, cinnamon and nutmeg.
- With a hand mixer, mix all of the ingredients together until it becomes very liquefied.
- Add your Raisins, nuts or drained crushed pineapples (if you desire).
- Mix all of the contents with a large mixing spoon and blend everything in until it is smooth.
- Pour batter evenly into both pie crusts.
- Bake at 325 degrees, evenly for 1 hour -1hour 20 min or until ready.
- Let cool for 20 mins and serve.

*Note that you can always bake them without any nuts or pineapple. Or you can make one pie crust with the nuts, the other pie crust with the pineapple. Or you can blend them both together either way the choice is totally up to you.

Freedom Pie

Freedom pie is a family tradition passed down from my great-grandmother. My great-grandmother taught my grandmother, who taught my mother, who taught my sisters and me. When we would visit my grandmother, she would share stories about how they escaped slavery and the cruelty inflicted on them. My great-grandmother's parents were slaves and freed when my grandmother Sophie was eight years old.

Grandma Sophie shared with us that she was already spoiled when she was freed from slavery, meaning she had already been taken advantage of sexually. She recalled her family traveling from place to place and hiding from the vigilantes in whatever abandoned huts they could find, escaping the possibilities of being captured, enslaved, or killed.

My great-grandfather kept the family fed as they journeyed through the fields at night. He would gather white potatoes, sugar cane, beans, and peas from nearby crops so my great-grandmother could prepare the meals. Her white potato pie became known as Freedom Pie because it symbolized his vow that he nor his family would ever go back into slavery. Not taking their freedom for granted, they moved with such care and strategy as they knew their freedom could be taken away in the blink of an eye.

Today, I prepare this dish every holiday in remembrance of my ancestors and the ultimate price they paid for freedom. In my opinion, each generation needs to embrace life and remember the sacrifices our ancestors made to be free and stay free. Who would have known freedom, a God-given right, would cause so much pain, separation, and heartbreak?

The raisins and pineapples of this pie represent the sweetness of life, and the nuts represent hardship. Let us not forget! I hope you enjoy it.

My Notes:

Church Cake

INGREDIENTS

- 4 Large Eggs
- 1 tsp. baking powder
- 1 tsp. baking soda
- 2 ¼ cups All-purpose flour
- 2 cups granulated sugar
- 1 tsp. Salt
- 2 tsp. vanilla flavor
- 1 cup butter
- ½ cup Milk
- ½ cup Sour cream, light or regular

DIRECTIONS

- In a small bowl whisk together, milk and sour cream.
- Make sure it is room temperature.
- Preheat your oven to 325 degrees.
- In a large bowl or electric stand mixer. Whip butter on medium speed for 1-2 minutes. Add granulated sugar and vanilla, whip again on medium speed for 4-5 min.
- Then add eggs one at a time, mix until all combined.
- In a fine mesh strainer add the flour, baking powder, baking soda and salt (dry mix).
- Sift them together.
- Gradually add the dry ingredients to the batter and mix well until combined.
- Add part of the milk/sour cream mixture to the batter and mix well.
- Then add the rest of the dry Mix along with the rest of milk and sour cream mixture.
- Be sure to spray the tube pan with cooking spray with flour very well.
- Divide the batter evenly around the tube pan.
- Be sure there are no air bubbles in your batter.
- Bake at 325 degrees for 45 min -1 hour or until lightly golden.
- Be sure to resist opening/closing your oven to check on your cake, this will cause your cake to fall.
- Let the cakes rest in the pan for 5-10mins before gently turning it over to a cooling rack to completely cool.

Church Cake

I remember waking up on a Sunday morning to the smell of cake baking. The aroma was so sweet that you could almost taste the cake through the scent. My sisters and I would jump up from excitement because we knew it was our mother's famous "Church Cake." It got its nickname because my mom would make this cake for the church congregation at least twice a month. We also referred to it as a "special cake" because she made it in a pot. Yes, that's right––a pot!

I remember my mother and other women setting up picnic tables outside the church on Sundays to display their homemade dishes. It was supposed to give people a cookout vibe, but it was more of a cooking contest for the ladies in my eyes. My mom would cook several different meals, but the church cake would always be the first to go. Everyone always inquired about the recipe, but my mother never shared it.

People's love for my mother's cooking made one lady at church dislike her. I would watch her staring angrily as the congregation gathered around my mother's table for a taste of her food. She never tried my mother's food for herself. I guess her pride wouldn't let her. She even had the nerve to compare her cake to my mother's. Poor baby!

Today, in memory of my mother, I make a church cake at least twice a month. The only difference is I use a Bundt pan, but it still comes out tasting the same–– delicious.

My Notes:

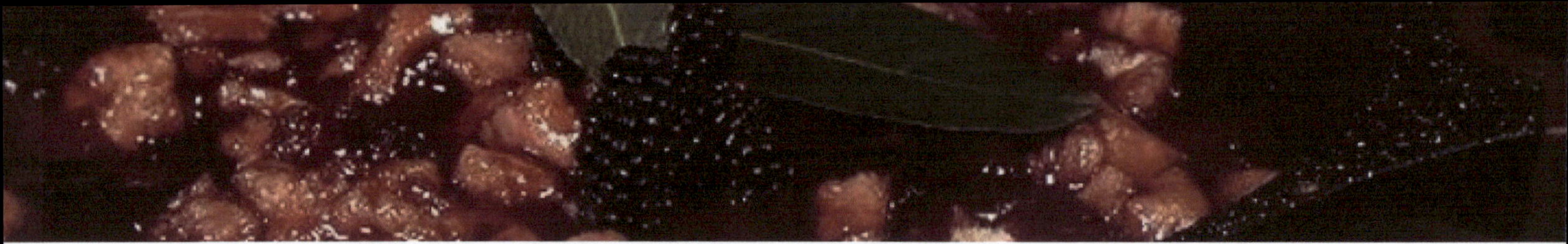

Blackberry Dumplings

"When we were younger, my sisters and I loved my mother's blackberry dumplings. The five of us–– Earthalean, Vern, Loretta, Deloris, and myself, would help by picking blackberries so she could make it"

INGREDIENTS

- DOUGH:
- ½ stick of butter
- ½ cup of blackberry liqueur
- ½ cup of water
- 1 ½ cups of self-rising flour
-
- BLACKBERRIES:
- 3 large packs of blackberries
- 1 tsp of cinnamon
- 2 tbsp of Butter
- 3 cups of blackberry Creme De Mure
- 1 ½ cup of water
- 1 cups of Sugar

DIRECTIONS

- Dough: In a medium sized bowl add your flour, ½ stick of butter (room temperature), sugar, water and blackberry liqueur.
- Mix together until the dough is stiff.
- Roll the dough very thinly with your rolling pin.
- Cut your dough into 1 ½ inch squares.
- Blackberries:
- In a medium size pot add all of your blackberries, butter, sugar, cinnamon, water, and blackberry creme de mure,
- Bring content to a boil for 25 minutes.
- Turn down to a medium/low flame
- Now drop your dumplings into your pot while folding it into the liquid.
- Once you have finished dropping your dough.
- Cover pot with a lid for 5 minutes
- Turn it off and let it rest for 5 minutes.
- serve!
- Note: this can be served with ice cream or pound cake.

Blackberry Dumplings

When we were younger, my sisters and I loved my mother's blackberry dumplings. The five of us–– Earthalean, Vern, Loretta, Deloris, and myself, would help by picking blackberries so she could make it. Before we skipped off into the fields, my mom would warn us, "Watch out for those snakes!" There were a lot of snakes in the fields. I guess they loved the blackberries as much as we did. Not only did we have to look out for snakes, but we also had to be careful of the thorns on the branches. The very sharp thorns sometimes made it difficult to grab the blackberries. After filling up our basket with berries, we would race home. Somehow, Vern was always the first to get back.

Despite being diagnosed with polio, Vern was the fastest of the five of us. She would win the foot race, but my mom always waited for all of us to return home before she started making her blueberry dumplings. Deloris, the baby, was the smallest and always finished last. But because she would cry loudly, I was led to believe her tears triggered Mom to pick from her basket first just to shut her up! After my mother gathered all our blackberries, we would line up in excitement and anticipation to watch her cook. Once it was done, she would allow us to have a small taste of it before dinner.

My mother's blackberry dumpling recipe is something that I have passed down to my children and my grandchildren. Even though they don't have to go to the fields to pick the berries, the love and fun in making this dish are still felt. Plus, the taste is so delightful!

My Notes:

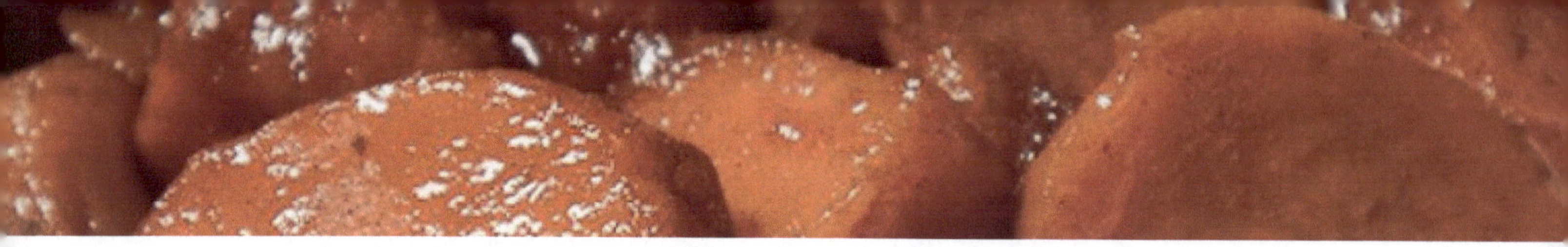

Candied Yams

INGREDIENTS

- 4 medium size potatoes
- ½ stick of butter
- 1 tbsp. of vanilla extract
- ½ cup of brown sugar
- 1 pinch of nutmeg
- 2 tbsp. of cinnamon
- 1 cup of syrup

DIRECTIONS

- Peel and cut your potatoes into circles.
- Place in a medium size pot and Boil sweet potatoes for 20 min, make sure it is still a little firm (Do not overcook your sweet potatoes).
- After your potatoes are done, strain them.
- In the large, preheated skillet place syrup, ½ stick of butter, and all of your ingredients (except brown sugar and cinnamon) over a medium flame.
- Then place your strained sweet potato in the skillet. Be sure to spread them out in the pan.
- Once it's in the pan sprinkle your brown sugar and cinnamon on top of the potatoes.
- Place a top on your sweet potatoes for about 8 min.
- Remove the top and flip the slices until the glaze is nice and thick.
- Once you have a thick glaze around your sweet potatoes, turn off your heat and allow the sweet potatoes to simmer for 5 min.
- Now your candied yams will be ready to serve.

Note: If you do not have the time to cook the candy yams on top of the stove, you can put all of your ingredients into a casserole dish and bake for 1 hour to 1 hour 20 min.

Sweet potatoes are a dish I have loved since I was a young girl, and I still enjoy them. I now share my love of them with my twelve grandchildren through a recipe I created to ensure they have the true essence of the meal and something healthy for them to eat.

You see, my dad grew sweet potatoes in our field. During the fall, he would come home with a sack full of sweet potatoes, and all of us would sit by the fireplace and watch as he placed the sweet potatoes in the hot coal. While the sweet potatoes were roasting, my dad would tell us stories, jokes, and poems. One story he shared is called "The Rebellious Pig." My dad would often say, "Some people are rebellious just like a pig." He would tell us these stories to stimulate our minds. I recite this same story to my children and grandchildren today.

There once was a farmer who had a pig, and the pig got out of his stall.

The farmer said, "Pig, get back in the stall!"

The pig said, "No."

So then the farmer said, "Dog, bite Pig and make the pig get back in his stall!"

The dog said, "No. Pig didn't do anything to me."

Then the farmer said, "Stick, hit Dog, make Dog bite Pig, and make Pig get back in his stall!"

Stick said, "No. The dog didn't do anything to me."

The farmer said, "Fire, burn Stick, make Stick hit Dog, make Dog bite Pig, and make Pig get back in his stall."

Fire replied, "No. Stick didn't do anything to me."

So, the farmer said, "Water, out Fire, make Fire burn Stick, make Stick hit Dog, make Dog bite Pig, and make Pig get back in his stall."

Water said, "No. Fire didn't do anything to me."

The farmer then said, "Ox, drink Water, make Water out fire, make Fire burn Stick, make Stick hit Dog, make Dog bite Pig, and make Pig get back in his stall."

The Ox said, "No. Water didn't do anything to me."

So, the farmer said, "Rope, hang Ox, make Ox drink Water, make Water out Fire, make Fire burn Stick, make Stick hit Dog, make Dog bite Pig, and make Pig get back in his stall."

Rope said, "No. Ox didn't do anything to me."

Then the farmer said, "Knife, cut Rope, make Rope hang Ox, make Ox drink Water, make Water out Fire, make Fire burn Stick, make Stick hit Dog, make Dog bite Pig, and make Pig get back in his stall."

The Knife said, "No. Rope didn't do anything to me."

The farmer then said, "Hammer, break Knife, make Knife cut Rope, make Rope hang Ox, make Ox drink Water, make Water out Fire, make Fire burn Stick, make Stick hit Dog, make Dog bite Pig, and make Pig get back in his stall."

By this time, we were anxiously waiting to hear how the pig got back in the stall. After a moment of silence, my dad took a deep breath before continuing the story:

Hammer began to break Knife. Knife began to cut Rope. Rope began to hang Ox. Ox began to drink Water. Water began to out Fire. Fire began to burn Stick. Stick began to hit Dog. Dog began to bite Pig, and Pig got back in his stall.

My dad would then look at us and say, "Now, repeat it."

Eventually, we were able to repeat it as fast as he did, but it took some time.

As he told us stories, I would glance at the fireplace. It always seemed as if there were little men made of fire dancing around on the coals. After an hour of my dad's storytelling, he would instruct us to grab a plate and gave each of us one of the sweet potatoes from the fireplace. They were the sweetest potatoes I have ever tasted. Man, that was the best time. Yum, yum, CANDIED YAMS!

My Notes:

"I need you to understand how everything my mother prepared was amazingly tasteful, especially her pies. My mother made the best pies in the world. They were so delicious that many of the neighbors would ask her to bake pies for them."

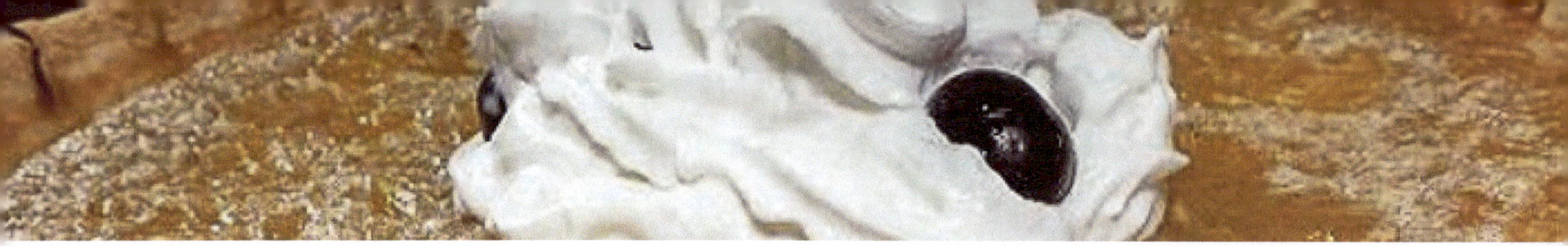

Cream Cheese Sweet Potato Pie

"Sweet potato pie has been around for years, and I'm sure it will remain one of my favorites."

INGREDIENTS

- ½ cup of cream cheese (softened)
- 1 cup of granulated sugar
- 4 Eggs
- 4 medium sweet potatoes
- ⅓ cup of heavy whipping cream
- ½ cups of brown sugar
- 1 tbsp. of cinnamon
- 1 pinch of ground nutmeg
- 1 pinch of salt
- 1 deep dish pie crust
- ½ stick of butter
- 1 tbsp. of vanilla flavoring

DIRECTIONS

- Place your sweet potatoes on a cookie sheet.
- Place your sweet potatoes in the oven at 375 degrees for 45 minutes to an hour or until very soft.
- After the sweet potatoes are done, let cool for 5 minutes.
- Peel your sweet potatoes and place them in a large bowl.
- Add your butter and your cream cheese into the bowl.
- Add your egg one at a time while mixing on medium speed.
- Add your cream cheese, cinnamon, salt, nutmeg, sugar, brown sugar, and vanilla flavoring.
- Mix on a high speed for 5 minutes.
- Place batter in your pie crust. Bake for 40 minutes.
- Note: This batter will be enough for 2 pies. Eat and enjoy my friends! Save a piece for me!

Cream Cheese Sweet Potato Pie

Sweet potato pie has been around for years, and I'm sure it will remain one of my favorites. By now, you are probably tired of me mentioning my mother's love for cooking, but I need you to understand how everything she prepared was amazingly tasteful, especially her pies. My mother made the best pies in the world. They were so delicious that many of the neighbors would ask her to bake pies for them. She would smile while baking pies to take to church or to serve to anyone who stopped by the house to enjoy them.

Just the smell of the sweet potatoes baking in the oven was enough to make your mouth water. As my mother prepared the pies, I watched closely, thinking in my little head that it was an easy dish to make. Having watched her make this pie more times than I can count, I had it down to a science. When I became a mother and started cooking for my family, I added a little twist to the recipe––cream cheese. Cream cheese became the secret ingredient and trust me when I say this pie is just what the doctor ordered.

Cream cheese became the secret ingredient and trust me when I say this pie is just what the doctor ordered.

My Notes:

Carrot Pie

INGREDIENTS

- 6 carrots
- 1 cups of brown sugar
- 1 ½ tbsp. of cinnamon
- ¼ tsp. of nutmeg
- 3 eggs
- 1 tsp. of vanilla flavoring
- 1 pinch of salt
- ⅓ cups of cream or milk
- 2 deep dish pie crust

"Mom-Mom, I want a carrot pie!" When I told my grandson that I didn't think there was such a thing, he replied, "Mom-Mom, you can make anything you put your mind to."

DIRECTIONS

- Cook carrots in water until tender.
- When carrots are tender, drain them.
- Place the carrots, brown sugar, cinnamon, nutmeg, eggs, vanilla flavoring, salt and milk into the blender.
- Blend until creamy.
- Place batter in the pie crust.
- Bake for 35 minutes at 350 Degrees.

Note: This batter will be enough for 2 pies. Eat and enjoy my friends!

Carrot Pie

While I was cutting carrots one day, my grandson said to me, "Mom-Mom, I want a carrot pie!" When I told him that I didn't think there was such a thing, he replied, "Mom-Mom, you can make anything you put your mind to." I would tell my children and grandkids this same thing, but I never imagined he would turn that saying around and use it on me. However, he was right! So, I bought some carrots and experimented.

The first time I made it, Braxton loved it. However, it fell short of satisfying his sister Brooke's taste buds. "Mom-Mom, will you please try again?" she asked. So, I decided to try again. The following week, I bought some more carrots and attempted once more to make a carrot pie. This time, it was delicious and received their approval!

This recipe for carrot pie was created by Mom-Mom but inspired by my grandchildren. Look at God!

My Notes:

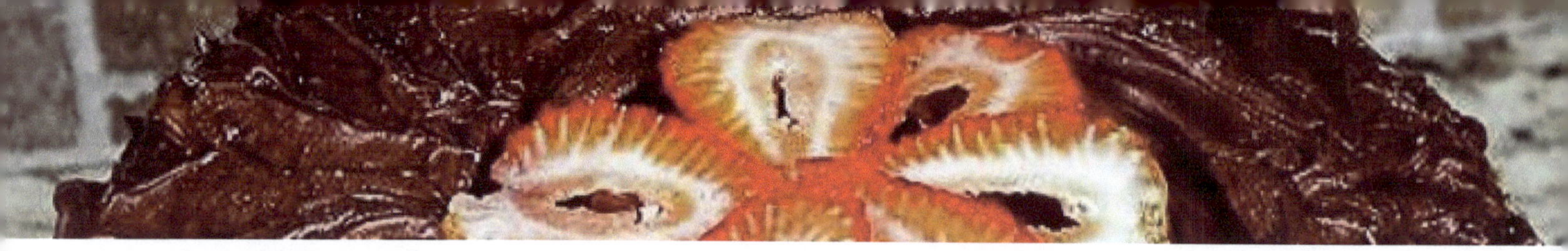

Semi-Sweet Chocolate Cake

INGREDIENTS

- 15lb Turkey
- ½ stick Butter
- ¼ cup olive oil
- 1 small onion
- 1 tbsp. sage
- 1 tbsp. salt
- 1 tbsp. pepper
- 1 tbsp. poultry seasoning

"This dessert is an old-fashioned classic in our family. "

DIRECTIONS

- Thaw Turkey overnight.
- Clean your turkey and please don't forget to take the bag from the inside of the turkey. Mix all seasonings together and sprinkle all over the turkey, don't forget the inside.
- Cut the onion in thin circles and place them inside the turkey.
- Place turkey in a roasting pan and bake for ½ hrs. per pound on 325 degrees.
- Turkey should be golden brown. Allow the turkey to rest 10-20mins before carving.

Semi-Sweet Chocolate Cake

This dessert is an old-fashioned classic in our family. My mom must've made this cake over five hundred times, but every time she did, everyone would get excited. Each time, it tasted better than the first.

When my mother made this, she would buy a big block of chocolate, and with a sharp knife, she cut and chiseled little pieces into a bowl. Nowadays, you can go to the market and buy a bag of chocolates, which saves time and less sweat in the kitchen. Maybe you'll experiment by tweaking the recipe and coming up with a new twist for this delectable cake.

Enjoy this classic. Better yet, share it with friends.

My Notes:

Sweet Potatoe Squares

"As you read in the other recipes, everyone loved sweet potatoes in our home, but sweet potato squares were my mother's favorite to make."

INGREDIENTS

- 4 medium size sweet potatoes
- 1 stick of butter (room temp)
- 1 tsp of nutmeg
- 1 tbsp. of cinnamon
- 1 ½ cups of brown sugar
- 1 tbsp of vanilla flavoring
- 3 eggs
- ⅓ cup of sour cream
- 1 cup of milk
- 1 ½ cup flour
- 1 cup of crushed pecans (optional)
- 1 cup of raisins (optional)

DIRECTIONS

- Start by baking your sweet potatoes on 350 degrees for 45 mins or until soft and tender. Once done, allow to cool off before peeling. (make sure they are a little warm still)
- In a medium-size bowl or electric mixer add butter, nutmeg, vanilla flavor, cinnamon, sugar and eggs
- Mash the sweet potatoes evenly as you mix well.
- Then add your sour cream, milk, and flour.
- (optional) you can also add crushed pecans or nuts of your choice and raisins.
- Be sure to mix everything evenly.
- Lightly spray your cookie sheet with oil.
- Next spread the batter evenly on the pan w/a spatula.
- Bake in the oven at 350 degrees for 40 min or until golden brown.
- Take it out, allow it cool for 15-20 min.
- Then cut into squares.
- And Enjoy

Sweet Potatoe Squares

As you read in the other recipes, everyone loved sweet potatoes in our home, but sweet potato squares were my mother's favorite to make. She would even add nuts, making them taste that much better. She made so many squares that my sisters and I would take a few across the road to less fortunate families. They loved my mom's squares as much as we did.

I remember being around ten years old and watching my mother make the squares in the hot kitchen. Oh my goodness, was it hot in there! Unfortunately, we didn't have an air conditioner, which was considered a luxury item back then. Despite the heat, watching my mother cook was always a great time and something I will never forget. It's one of the biggest reasons why I love to cook today. Mom would hum and smile while cooking or baking, and she would be at peace––like she had no cares or worries in the world. It was therapeutic, and she cooked with so much love. I believe that's what made her food and desserts taste so good.

Every time I cook, I think back to when I watched my mom cooking with love, and it brings me great joy. So, Mom, these sweet potato squares are for you. Love you!

My Notes:

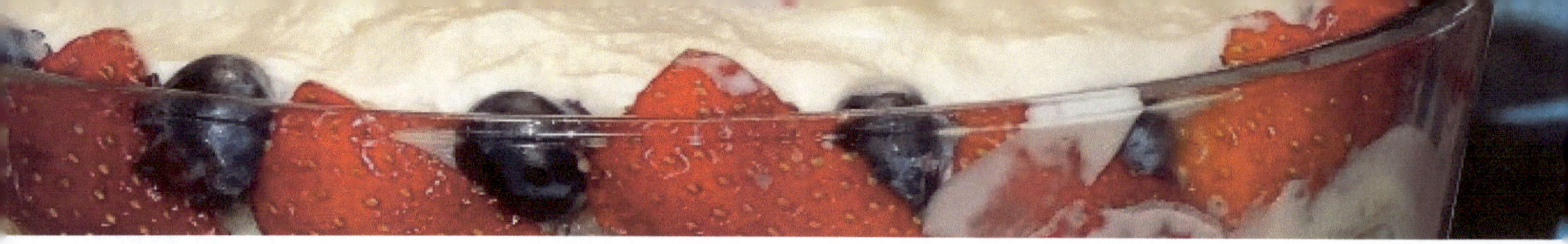

Look At God Cake

"My perspective of God and realizing His power inspired me to give Him all the glory, honor, and praise."

INGREDIENTS

(Fruit)

- 1 box of yellow cake mix
- 1 can of pie filling- peaches
- 1 can of pie filling -apples
- 1 can of pie filling- cherries
- 1 can of pie filling- pineapples
- 4 bananas
- 1 small container of blueberries
- 1 small container of strawberries

(Pudding)

- 1 large pack of vanilla pudding

DIRECTIONS

(Cake)

- **Get one box of yellow cake mix, follow the instructions on the cake box.**

(Pudding)

- **Use one large pack of vanilla pudding, follow the directions on the box.**

(Putting it all together)

- **Once your cake is cooled, cut the cake in half and place the bottom half of the cake in your trifle bowl.**
- **Pour a layer of pudding over the cake.**
- **Start placing the fruit in your trifle bowl.**
- **Place the peaches around the cake until it is completely covered, followed by your apples, blueberries, strawberries, drained pineapples, cherries and bananas.**
- **Don't forget that you're layering this cake so be mindful to save enough for the other layers.**

Look At God Cake

When I was eight years old, my mother sent me to the store to purchase a loaf of bread. When I entered the store, I noticed a parrot in the back. As I walked around picking up my items, the parrot began quoting racial slurs towards me, but it would not utter a word when other patrons picked up their merchandise. Then I was faced with waiting. How could I be the first patron in the store and the last to be serviced? That whole experience left me crushed. I walked home feeling worthless as tears fell from my eyes.

Once I got home, I walked into the kitchen where my mother was cooking and handed her the loaf of bread. Seeing my tears, she knelt on one knee, kissed the tears on my face, and asked, "Baby, what's wrong?"

"Mom, why are there so many people greater than me?" I asked after sharing my experience with her.

While looking me in the eyes, my mother replied, "Baby, there is no one greater than you except God."

What she said at that moment changed my whole life. My perspective of God and realizing His power inspired me to give Him all the glory, honor, and praise. When anything profound happened in my life, I would say, "Look at God!" This phrase allowed me to respect our differences while appreciating His grace.

When I first made this dessert years ago, I connected the different types of fruit, colors, and layers of the cake to represent the people who make up society. Today, this cake reminds me of God's grace and the twelve blessings I call my grandchildren: Ashlee, Eric, Lauren, Kevin Jr., Michael III, Caleb, Konhrad, Denim, Diezel, Braxton, Brooke, and Logan.

Over the years, I have come to realize that everything is done in

God's divine order.

Look at GOD!

My Notes:

THANK YOU FOR
Cooking with Ms. E

Acknowledgements

Giving honor to God, my Creator, my Lord and Savior Jesus Christ, and Holy Spirit who dwells within me.

I dedicate this book to my parents, Reverend John J. and Beulah Jackson. You are the reason I am the woman who I have become today. To my sisters, Vernaree Harrison and DeLois Gordon, thank you for standing by my side, praying for me, and encouraging me no matter what. Dr. Eugene "Uncle Matt" and Vermel "Auntie Vee" Matthews, you have been my counselors and have empowered me in so many ways. To Leon and Barbara Oldham, the greatest "brother and sister" anyone could have. The gratitude and love I have for you are indescribable.

To my six amazing children: Toni, Michael, Traci, Towanda, Trina, and Tamar. Thank you for being the greatest children, sharing in my happiness with this project, and helping me through so much. To my twelve grandchildren: Ashlee, Lauren, Eric, Michael, Kevin II, Caleb, Denim, Diezel, Konrad, Braxton, Brooke, and Logan, and of course, my very first great-grandchild, Kevin III. You are all the sunshine of my life and the apple of my eye.

To my friends and confidants: Judge Mablean Ephriam, Drs. Victor and Sherry Blake, Judge Larry and Joyce Mimms, Attorney Toni Moore, Esq., Attorney Antavious Weems, Gilda Weaver, Ernestine Love, and Ruby Lucas. Thank you all for being there and for lending your listening ear.

To Bishop Eusebio and Laurona Phelps, Bishop Williams Shields, and Apostle Craig Coates, thank you for your continued prayers.

A special thanks to Michalea Bennett, Shaniece Turner, and Lakisha Ross for your commitment, dedication, time, and love. Audra Howard, Gregory Moore, LaVonté Dove, Charron Monaye, and Michael Witherspoon, thank you for being so wonderful.

Finally, I want to thank everyone––near and far––who has supported me on my life's journey. Life has indeed not been a crystal stair, but through the grace of God and the favor bestowed upon my life, I am still here. This book is truly a labor of love and just the appetizer of who I truly am. So, stay tuned because there is always more, as this is only the beginning.

I Love You ...
LOOK AT GOD!

About The Author

Evelyn Braxton wears many hats––minister, life coach, singer, and matriarch to America's talented siblings, Toni, Michael, Traci, Towanda, Trina, and Tamar Braxton. Ms. Braxton comes fully armed with her love of God and her educational background to inspire people worldwide. From the long roads of Columbia, South Carolina, to the city streets of Severn, Maryland, Ms. Braxton quickly learned the value of family and a solid foundation with God. After facing and overcoming the hardships that life can bring, Ms. Braxton has learned to live with no regrets. Instead, she lives a life full of love and grace.

Ms. Braxton is committed to serving others, recently launching several businesses created to encourage and inspire that it is never too late to believe in yourself and follow your dreams. Ms. Braxton is the founder of God Can Heal the Heart, an organization of self-development founded to edify and counsel individuals towards their true purpose in life. From witnessing domestic abuse, depression, and overcoming personal struggles, Ms. Braxton is now using her platform to advocate for and with individuals who want to have a better life. Ms. Braxton doesn't stop there. She has launched her own beauty line, Ms. E's Beauty Solutions, a beauty brand created to enhance one's natural beauty. Ms. E's Eyebrow Growth Serum conditions and enhances for fuller, healthier-looking brows.

Today, Ms. Braxton is working on adding the title of author to her resume. She is preparing, with great excitement, for the release of her debut book, Cooking with Ms. E: A Book of Recipes and Family Memoirs. This cookbook is both a culinary and a personal memoir of Ms. Braxton's life. This project is very near and dear to Ms. Braxton's heart, offering a connection to her love of cooking and her family.

Evelyn Braxton attended Sojourner College (Annapolis, MD) and Bowie State University (Bowie, MD), where she studied Social Science and Psychology. She also attended Wesley Seminary College in Washington, D.C. In addition, she was a volunteer counselor at Sarah's House of Distressed Women and Family Shelter. Ms. Braxton enjoys sharing life nuggets, along with spending time with her children, grandchildren, and great-grandson.

CPSIA information can be obtained
at www.ICGtesting.com
Printed in the USA
BVHW022141211021
619618BV00007B/114

* 9 7 8 1 6 8 5 6 4 2 8 7 7 *